ACCLAIM FOR
The Desecrators

"The unraveling of America is now at a furious pace, and this is just the book to capture what has been happening and why. Unlike reformers of the past, today's activists seek not to improve but to tear down: their anarchist thumbprints are everywhere apparent. Both of the authors have had a distinguished career in politics and in Catholic circles, and the poignant anecdotes they share gives the book a personal touch. They cover much ground, and they do it with considerable flair."

—Bill Donohue, PhD, president, Catholic
League for Religious and Civil Rights

"Matt Schlapp and Deal Hudson perceptively read the moment and expose the nature of the threats to foundational American and human ideals, including the assault on life itself and the most innocent among us. There is no one better to outline where we're headed and how the obstacles can be successfully overcome than these two visionary men of faith, who so generously share their insight. *The Desecrators* is filled with both urgency and vital hope for the America future generations will inherit."

—Marjorie Dannenfelser, president,
Susan B. Anthony List

"In this must-read book, Matt Schlapp and Deal Hudson analyze what Yale law professor Stephen L. Carter once called 'the culture of disbelief' and Richard John Neuhaus decried as the 'naked public square.' The systematic attempt to marginalize people of faith and thereby undermine America's Judeo-Christian foundations is not new, but its codification as cancel culture is. The authors urge that we reaffirm the faith of our founders and, most critically, provide a realistic plan to win."

—Ralph Reed, political consultant

"If you want to know how to live as a patriotic Christian American today, fully aware of the dangers of our times and yet strengthened by hope, *The Desecrators* is the book to read. It will ground you in reality; it will make you want to jump up and fight for what is right; it will challenge you, in the spirit of the Founders and of the martyrs, to give your all for America and for the Gospel!"

—Fr. Frank Pavone, national director, Priests for Life
president, National Pro-life Religious Council

THE
DESECRATORS

Defeating the Cancel Culture Mob and
Reclaiming One Nation Under God

Matt Schlapp
&
Deal W. Hudson

TAN Books
Gastonia, North Carolina

Library of Congress Control Number: 2021950429
ISBN: 978-1-5051-2009-7
Kindle ISBN: 978-1-5051-2010-3
ePUB ISBN: 978-1-5051-2011-0

Published in the United States by
TAN Books
PO Box 269
Gastonia, NC 28052
www.TANBooks.com

To Mom who is my Hero
& to Mercy who is my Heart
—Matt Schlapp

To Theresa C. Hudson for more than thirty years
—Deal W. Hudson

Contents

Foreword

The idea for *The Desecrators* started on our front porch where Matt and I would drink our morning cup of coffee. Our conversation always led to discussion about the declining state of affairs in America. We felt that we weren't the only ones sitting on the front porch looking to the horizon and feeling that we were losing this great country. We were in the middle of the horrific COVID-19 pandemic where thousands of Americans, especially older Americans, had died. Many Americans were living in fear, socially distancing themselves from their families, and being yelled at by their neighbors for not wearing a mask. The stress and anxiety was escalating, and any sense of normalcy had ended in our communities and churches.

The world looked grim. Rising deaths, endless lockdowns, and closed schools only added to the heartache. And the government's response is more control: mask mandates, vaccine mandates, lockdowns, and school shutdowns—all in the name of the COVID. We were also living in a new woke world where chaos and confusion were penetrating every aspect of our lives and directly impacting our children. It seemed like the darkness and sadness would never end. Matt and I could only hold on to our faith, our family, and each other. We found ourselves praying the Rosary every night with the family and asking for wisdom and God's mercy on our country.

Politically, the Republicans were lost after the 2020 election. Many of us were bullish about President Trump winning the presidential election. Matt and I traveled around the country and met thousands of Americans who all saw the dangers of the ambient spirit of socialism permeating their communities. We felt hopeless on election night, and with President Joe Biden now in the White House, anyone associated with President Donald J. Trump was considered evil by the Left and liberal media. Matt was the subject of a targeted campaign by the Left to destroy his business and our lives. The assault by the Left was fierce, with the goal of silencing Matt for his attempt to expose Marxist organizations shielded by the Left. Many corporations caved to the Left and bowed down to their every demand. But Matt would never cave. It was painful for me to watch how Matt was constantly attacked and targeted, and at times, our children and I were also attacked on social media. It was scary. During the campaign, an execution list was shared on social media on which several of us from the campaign were named. The Never Trump movement's Lincoln Project created the list of Trump people not to hire—I was included. I had never witnessed such vicious and destructive political behavior. It was pure evil and hate. At one point, I told Matt we needed to get out of the public eye, but I knew that we had been called to speak up for those afraid to speak. He would not back down despite the price, and he stood determined to fight against government control and the socialist agenda taking root in our communities.

Deal Hudson joined us on the front porch for several sessions and dissected the current problems in our society and the Church. Matt and I have known Deal for over twenty years, going back to the George W. Bush days. He is a level-headed philosopher and critical and common-sense thinker. I have always admired his ability to explain the intricacies of our Catholic faith and the unique moment in which we live. His calm demeanor juxtaposes Matt's feisty and energetic nature. Writing a book is a daunting task, and Deal guided Matt every step of the way. It was a critical time to write the blueprint for reclaiming America, and I knew combining the political and philosophical minds of Matt and Deal would create a meaningful and impactful book for those in search of inspiration and hope for our country.

Venerable Sister Lucia, one of the seers from Fatima, once wrote, "From now on, we are either with God or we are with the Devil; there is no middle ground."[1] We have arrived at a moment that cries for a decision about who we stand with and who we defend. Institutions are failing us, and it falls to the people and faithful to save this country. The Desecrators have spent their time fomenting chaos and confusion and dividing us by race and an assault on gender. With the school shutdowns, many parents saw firsthand the insanity of the Left's propaganda being taught in their children's classes. Because of COVID-19 and ill-advised government and school policy decisions, our children lost their youth, their dreams, and their relationships. They suffered tremendous pain and mental health issues that could take a lifetime to heal.

---

[1] Augustin Fuentes, "Sister Lucy's Last Public Interview-1957," Tradition in Action, accessed November 8, 2021, https://www.traditioninaction.org/HotTopics/g23ht_Interview.html.

The government and the liberal media created unnecessary panic and fear that drove us all to avoid contact with others. The madness felt like it would never end. With the country in the hands of a mentally unfit president, a propaganda machine, social media, and with progressives in charge, we are headed in the wrong direction. While the Desecrators seek to take control of our lives, we have found a way to push back and not accept the lies of the Left. We remember a time when we pledged allegiance to the American flag using the words "under God" and taught our children what the flag stands for: freedom. We cherish our freedom to speak up, our freedom to worship, and our freedom to pursue happiness, and we need to stop the Desecrators. Freedoms are fragile and must be protected by each and every one of us.

Americans have proven that they are courageous and resilient. We have seen the rise of parents, everyday moms and dads who have taken on the Desecrators who have targeted their children. It moves me to tears watching these parents speak up at the school board meetings and challenge the destructive public school systems. Their bravery has changed the political landscape. They inspire us all that every voice matters and that we the people are in charge—not the Leftist mob.

As we would tell our children, in the darkness there is light. Where there are Desecrators, there are saints and everyday heroes who believe in the goodness and glory of God and will be responsible for saving America. The Desecrators will fail because God is in charge and the devil will be defeated. There is no middle ground. One day, Americans will gather with their loved ones on the front porch with a sense of hope and victory. They will recall the days of darkness and know that their voices made all the difference in reclaiming a nation once bereft of hope.

—Mercedes Schlapp

Acknowledgments

This was my first attempt at writing a book, and it would have been impossible without Deal Hudson. He is a great man and faithful friend who always has the discernment to be on the right side of meaningful battles.

My soul needed an outlet that allowed me to think more intensely than in a TV interview and be able to relay what I believe God is calling righteous people to do: fight now, no matter how much personal risk it might require. The America we cherish could crumble, and with it, the core freedoms around the globe that America impacts, starting with religious freedom.

Of course, my wife is my partner in life and professionally. It seems we are always each other's top advisor, and sometimes each other's boss. Mercy is the sweetest, most loyal, and most fierce woman I have ever met. My love for her deepens as my respect for her character grows. I am sorry, Sweetie, that I still don't salsa very well.

I dedicated this book to Mercy, but also to my mom, Sue. She has always been my rock in a family confronted with obstacles and tragedy. Mom always got up and got through it no matter how embarrassing or tough the day was. And she always had a wry jab to make us all laugh and mock the insanity around her. Laughter was probably her second great gift to her kids (her strong faith gets the trophy). It was

Mom who taught me life was more challenge than celebration but that God would never abandon us and His plan for us was always for the good of His creation. She also taught me about life as she taught me competitive tennis. I cannot properly explain how much her lessons on the court translate into life in the arena: keep calm, be aggressive but patient, watch the ball and your opponent, always stay on your toes, take charge of the net whenever possible, and never play the score, because you can stage a comeback no matter how far you are down. I never won Wimbledon, and too often, I was a poor loser, but we all know our cause is greater than all that. The America we love is very far behind in the score; we just need to follow Mom's advice, starting now.

Mercy and I are blessed with a big, boisterous, loving family, all of whom support our work and are there for us, especially during the last five years. Mercy's father is constantly on our minds as he had the courage to fight Castro in Cuba and now worries about Castroism in America. We love our Florida Family: Lela, Abu, Melissa, Bob, Jose, Aimee; and our Kansas Clan: Andy, Jane, Carol, Jimmie, Chrissy, and Jason, and we adore all your kids. We are sorry for the times when you bear the brunt of what we say or do.

Thanks for all our dear friends from the two White House tours and in the Swamp who still put up with us, like Jana and Michael. Your numbers have dwindled, but as Mom always said, those who abandon you when you do right were never really your friends to begin with. Thanks to Stephen, Angela, and Frank, who help us so diligently at Cove Strategies. And to all our friends in the clergy who pray for us and encourage us, especially our pastor, Fr. Edward Hathaway; we need your support more than ever.

To all those who support CPAC, you have my enduring love and appreciation. CPAC has played a large role in the great battle of America versus Socialism, and we have given hope throughout the world to those committed to freedom and dignity. To the staff and the board and all the supporters, dedicating my public life to this cause has been my greatest professional honor.

Finally, to our five daughters: Viana, Caterina, Elissa, Ava, and Lucia, too often I have had to explain how regretful I am that my generation is handing you a society that glorifies the trends that are making things worse. All of us should have spoken up sooner and done more for the students of today. Your Mom and Dad are, with Diana's assistance, dedicated to engaging in this great struggle to cleanse the soul of America. We are striving to save a new generation from the confusion and pain resulting from the embrace of the false gods of the government knowing best all the time in all things and the chaos-inducing trendsetters who spin the allure of chic evil. We are doing this for you, and each of you motivate us every day to do our job right. You inspire us with your innocence and love. Thanks for reminding us that it is never too late to right a wrong or to answer the call.

Finally, a whole group of wonderful Kansans helped pay large portions of my tuition bills when my Dad died during my time at the University of Notre Dame. To each of you, some of whom have passed, I know that without your help, I would have faced desperation. I'll never forget each of you, nor Kapaun Mt. Carmel's own Sister Kathleen, who was a good nun but an even better fundraiser. May the prayers of Father Kapaun be with each one of you, and with this great country for which he gave his life.

With deep gratitude,
Matt Schlapp

I would like to thank those friends whose personal, intellectual, and spiritual guidance provided the foundation and perspective of this book: Bob Reilly, Jeff Wallin, Frank Buckley, Marjorie Dannenfelser, Claire Smith, Jeff Cavins, Deacon Keith Fournier, Msgr. Richard Lopez, Frank Hanna III, and David Hanna.

—Deal W. Hudson

Introduction

1.

We felt compelled to write this book because the country we pledge allegiance to and the truths to which we adhere are being attacked by evil forces that hate both America and our Church. Our country was formed in the crucible of a Christian culture. No nation on earth should be a better compliment to many of the moral teachings that shaped the Western world.

From her founding documents, America affirmed that the human person was created by God. This bestows on all of us rights that cannot be taken away by any temporal power—they are unalienable. All persons are therefore set apart from other creatures and things because we bear the stamp of God's creative will and love.

For half a century, people of faith have seen traditional ideas of morality undermined as a cascade of progressive revolutions impacted society. The waves of change hit the shores, but most nevertheless believed that families, the Church, truth, and education would all weather the storm.

But we were overconfident. We fought, but we also rested in the confidence that common sense and decency would prevail. It was impossible, it seemed, that the basic values held by our parents and grandparents would ever be challenged by charges of racism and, for many, their "whiteness."

Each day now brings news that defies common sense; it's as if the world has turned upside down and none of the old verities matter anymore.

When a society begins to unwind, chaos ensues. It's now crystal clear that our opponents want to create confusion, undermine basic truths, and take down America.

The opponents can be recognized by what they want to tear down: the family, traditional morality, gender, public order, public safety, police protection, freedom of speech, religious liberty, abortion restrictions, the military, America, Israel, and the Christian religion—an all-out assault on Western civilization

What name shall we give those nihilists? Let's call them the desecrators. These pathways of destruction described above are all acts of desecration; they are attacking, and in some cases removing, what we as people of faith and Americans consider sacred. The sacred is that which we value above all else; it refers directly to God or to our core principles. What else is the removal of a cross from a public place? Or the removal of a statue of an American war hero? Or taking God's holy name out of the pledge of allegiance? Or the accusation that America is inherently racist? Or the accusation that Christianity undergirds oppressive structures like marriage, the family, the rights of parents to education their children, and the priority of God's law over man's?

Thus far, we have witnessed desecration and destruction of statues of the likes of Saint Junípero Serra, Saint Louis, Christopher Columbus, Frederick Douglass, Abraham

Lincoln, Ulysses S. Grant, Thomas Jefferson, and even numerous statues of the Blessed Mother. Not a single statue of Saint Junípero Serra at the missions he founded in California has been left untouched. He was the missionary who literally brought Christianity to California.

Desecration has taken the form of cancel culture—the attack on the history, traditions, and moral principles that have shaped America. The desecrators also employ the power of public shaming to destroy the lives of those heroic individuals who dare to challenge them.

The people of faith in America must stop the systemic desecration being inflicted by our most powerful public institutions—from the media and schools to universities and elected governments—and we must strive in particular to restore the safety of a mother's womb.

2.

Since our founding, America has been foremost among nations in defending and promulgating liberty and human rights.

Those who promote and defend human rights around the globe rely on American support and leadership. They are concerned that if America becomes another run-of-the-mill secular democracy embracing socialism, its fight for freedom in smaller countries will dissipate.

President Donald J. Trump was a leader who recognized the human dignity of the unborn child, the unemployed, the poor, the unjustly imprisoned, and all those struggling to make ends meet. He understood there were forgotten men and women of America and across the globe whose plight was being ignored by the powerful. These decent people pray that America remains strong so she can continue to speak up for their intrinsic dignity and God-given rights.

In decades past, radicals have risen to prominence in America, but usually they were rejected or ignored if they hated America or promoted violence. The election of Barack Obama changed all that, and not for the better: anti-American radicalism was more aggressively embraced in the media, the universities, and public schools. The creation and wide acceptance of the *New York Times*'s "1619 Project" (2019) was made possible by the Obama presidency. This project claimed America was created to protect slavery. The *Times* itself explains the project's objective: "to reframe the country's history by placing the consequences of slavery . . . at the very center of our national [American] narrative." Most of us, including most of white America, hoped the first president of color would bring racial healing. His style of leadership appeared calming, but his harsh, leftist policies reinstated the racial polarization of the 1950s.

Throughout both his terms, Obama steadily pushed a theme that America had to be transformed due to its racist past. Obama set the stage for the "Great American Reset."[1]

Eight years of the Obama presidency helped millions of Americans understand that socialism and soft anti-Americanism would make them poorer, sicker, less optimistic of their personal futures, and more dubious that America would always persevere. This explains the unexpected

---

[1]   Llewellyn King, "King: The Great American Reset is underway, will change everything," *Boston Herald*, April 2, 2021, https://www.bostonherald.com/2021/04/02/king-the-great-american-reset-is-underway-will-change-everything/.

groundswell of support for Donald Trump in 2016, who, as everyone knows, wanted to "Make America Great Again."

We believe that groundswell still exists and will grow larger during the full reveal of the Biden presidency. Regardless of the reasons that President Joe Biden became president, his administration has already stoked the fires that previously led to Donald Trump's term in office.

3.

The desecrators came to power long before the Trump presidency. Donald Trump's four years in office gave him the chance to slow them down and push them back, but what is taken away can be given back, which is exactly what the new administration is rapidly doing.

The policies of the desecrators are an attempt to destroy the backbone of American culture and its commerce: decreasing the production of American fossil fuels, increasing taxes, regulating everything except abortion, educating our children to hate the land of their birth, destroying clear gender distinctions, helping Iran and other radical Islamic terrorists while weakening Israeli security interests, encouraging globalism while undermining the US military, coddling a rising Communist China and an untrustworthy Russia.

But even more damaging is the death star strategy the desecrators have built in an attempt to destroy any vestige of mom, apple pie, and the America we once knew. These forces are intent on ending the influence of traditional morality, the primacy of the family, and respect for all human life.

We know this because, with the rise of Black Lives Matter Inc. (BLM), we saw the left become so confident that it

actually published on its website its true intentions: socialism, the end of Israel, the nuclear family, Western churches,
economic profit, and a constitutionally-based America.[2]

Those who took over BLM and became its loudest voice
had the open intention to destroy the family was quickly
taken off its website but can still be seen in archives of its
pages. It declared, "We seek to disrupt the Western-prescribed
nuclear family structure requirement by supporting each
other as extended families and 'villages' that collectively care
for one another, especially our children, to the degree that
mothers, parents, and children are comfortable."[3]

The desecrators seek to disrupt and have no real intention
to make anyone "comfortable." They intend to end America
as we know it through the tactic of cancel culture, which aims
to not just register opposition to traditionalist policies but to
use elite power through media, foundations, and academia
to destroy the reputation of anyone who stands in their way.

The cancel culture worldview is the exact opposite of the
Judeo-Christian traditions and America's founding principles. Why? Because our faith is rooted in the past, in history, in time, and in time-tested truths. To cancel the past
is to forget all of salvation history, the Scriptures, the life of
Christ, and the body of the Church.

---

[2]   Melissa Chan, "Black Lives Matter Realeases List of Demands for
the First Time," *Time*, August 1, 2016, https://news.yahoo.com/bl
ack-lives-matter-releases-list-190056794.html.

[3]   Jon Miltimore, "Black Lives Matter's Goal to 'Disrupt' the Nuclear Family Fits a Marxist Aim That Goes Back a Century and
a Half," *FEE*, September 24, 2020, https://fee.org/articles/black
-lives-matter-s-goal-to-disrupt-the-nuclear-family-fits-a-marxist
-aim-that-goes-back-a-century-and-a-half/.

In other words, we lose the truth revealed to us—not just as it was once long ago but the truth as proclaimed for centuries. Our faith, our worldview, and our salvation depend upon awareness and affirmation of the past. These are sacred to us.

4.

The desecrator's worldview targets the foundational elements of society as shaped by the Judeo-Christian tradition, beginning with the family. Why the family? The family is the crucible of human development. The family is where the truth of the past is carried forward through children and grandchildren.

Each human person receives his or her most important nurturing in the first years of life. Virtues, values, and worldviews are all learned during these years.

Catholics, other Christians, and other people of faith in America should be deeply alarmed about the ongoing attacks. The desecrators are even accusing the first chapter in Holy Scripture of causing "hatred." Why? In part, because the chapter contains this line: "So God created man in his own image, in the image of God he created him; male and female he created them" (Gn 1:27).

The Democrats have proposed legislation that officially denies the truth of only two genders, male and female. The Equality Act (HR 5), if passed, will make the profession of this truth punishable under law.[4] But this proposed legislation only starts with a redefinition of gender, which in itself

---

4   "11 Myths About H.R. 5, the Equality Act of 2021," The Heritage Foundation, February 24, 2021, https://www.heritage.org/gender /report/11-myths-about-hr-5-the-equality-act-2021.

is an attack on the Judeo-Christian tradition. It should be called the Desecration Act!

One Jewish commentator, Yaakov Menken, has called the Equality Act "a new era of government-sanctioned anti-religious bigotry."[5] He explains that some Jewish events are traditionally held in venues where men and women are separated. This legislation requires the "desegregation of public facilities [by] sex (including sexual orientation and gender identity)." In other words, centuries-old Jewish custom must change or be liable to federal prosecution. And that's only a single example.

Marriage itself as understood in Scripture and the Western tradition is regarded as a "sex stereotype" in the Equality Act, along with any judgments made on the basis of "gender identity" between male and female.[6]

One of the most frightening passages of HR 5 is this line overriding the protection of religious freedom: "The Religious Freedom Restoration Act of 1993 shall not provide a claim concerning, or a defense to a claim under, a covered title, or provide a basis for challenging the application or enforcement of a covered title."[7]

This bill goes way beyond allowing anyone who declares himself or herself being "female" access to the ladies'

5   Yaakov Menken, "How The Equality Act Would Legalize Religious Bigotry," *The Federalist*, March 23, 2021, https://thefedera list.com/2021/03/23/the-equality-act-would-legalize-religious-bi gotry/.

6   Ibid.

7   Mary Margaret Olohan, "Here's What's In The Equality Act," *Daily Caller*, February 25, 2021, https://dailycaller.com/2021/02 /25/the-equality-act-lgbtq-transgender-democrats/.

bathroom or locker room. The language makes it illegal for doctors to refuse to perform abortions.[8]

In the Equality Act, we see the federal government dictating a new worldview, starting with a radical ideology that separates sexuality and gender from nature and the physical reality of the body. That ideology will be pushed through public schools starting with kindergarten through sixth grade, meaning that parents will have to fight it out with the schools or find schools where the propaganda does not exist. Whether this legislation passes or not, it represents how a powerful minority of political and cultural elites want to "reset" our nation.

It's no surprise then that the legislation impacts faith-based adoption and foster care agencies where boys are still considered boys and girls are still considered girls. The state regulation of these agencies will be changed, requiring the acceptance of the new sexual ideology.[9] The Equality Act bases its power to enforce the new ideology by amending the 1964 Civil Rights Act to prohibit "discrimination" on the basis of sexual orientation and gender identity. Chief among the discriminatory practices is using a "sex stereotype" such as that taught in Genesis 1.[10]

[8]   Alexandra Desanctis, "The Equality Act Would Require Government-Funded Abortion," *National Review*, February 25, 2021, https://www.nationalreview.com/2021/02/the-equality-act-would-require-government-funded-abortion/.

[9]   Jeff Johnston, "'Equality Act' Discriminates Against Faith-based Adoption Agencies," *The Daily Citizen*, March 26, 2019, https://dailycitizen.focusonthefamily.com/equality-act-discriminates-against-faith-based-adoption-agencies/.

[10]   Ibid.

Whether the Equality Act passes or not, America's children and teenagers are already taking drugs and undergoing surgery to change their natural gender by the countless thousands.[11]

It's important to keep in the back of your mind that plans to abolish the family were made far in advance of BLM. Karl Marx, writing from the comfort of his London home, declared, "Abolish the family! . . . The bourgeois family will vanish as a matter of course when its complement vanishes, and both will vanish with the vanishing of capital."[12]

5.

The desecrators deliberately promote sexual confusion, particularly among children who are totally vulnerable to their manipulation. They say it's done in the name of freedom and choice. But the real target is nature, the nature described in the book of Genesis: "male and female he created them."

Destroy the two-gender worldview and you eventually destroy what the family was intended to be and what it was intended to accomplish for children.

In short, the desecrators treat the meaning of life as an empty blackboard upon which elites can redefine gender, family, community, politics, and truth. The important conservative philosopher Robert Nisbet put it this way: "Man

---

[11] Jeff Johnston, "Hospitals and Doctors 'Transition' Hundreds of Children with Drugs, Hormones and Surgery," *The Daily Citizen*, September 23, 2019, https://dailycitizen.focusonthefamily.com /hospitals-and-doctors-transition-hundreds-of-children-with-dru gs-hormones-and-surgery/.

[12] Karl Marx and Frederick Engels, *The Communist Manifesto*, Novemeber 2006, p. 24: http://www.slp.org/pdf/marx/comm_man .pdf.

is a social being, and his desire for community will not be denied. The liberated individual is just as likely to become the alienated individual, the paranoid individual, the lonely and desperately-seeking-community individual. And if he can't find that community on a human scale, then he'll look for it on an inhuman scale—in the total community of the totalizing state."[13]

This is precisely what is happening.

6.

How the desecrators use their power to end the careers and the reputations of cynics is aptly called the new inquisition. We have been taught how power corrupts over generations, and one of the most common examples to use is that of a powerful Catholic Church which silenced opposition with all the means at its disposal, including ending reputations, torture, and death.

The Catholic Church officially condemned her own past atrocities, but we cannot escape discussing them. Leave it to the woke Left in America to only mimic one aspect of Catholic history that suits its determination to transform society, the Inquisition.

This intolerant push by modern radicals is to entice us to accept any form of immorality while accepting no form of forgiveness. In other words, anything goes, but you will be condemned if you question those overseeing the destruction of societal order.

---

[13] Robert Nisbet, *The Quest for Community: A Study in the Ethics of Order and Freedom* (Wilmington, DE: Intercollegiate Studies Institute, 2010), loc. 74 of 6565, Kindle.

Persons who are found heretical by the woke court of this new inquisition are sentenced to a virtual death. This virtual death (or digital death) leads to loss of reputation, loss of jobs, loss of family and friends, and shame.

The new inquisition employs its desecrating minions to scour social media to identify heretics and prosecute them. The mainstream media enables the new inquisition by publicizing the heretic's name and his crime, thus ensuring that the punishment is a life sentence: the digital gulag.

The desecrators, like self-appointed oligarchs, set the rules, and they pick the inquisitors who decide who violates them. Everyone, including the powerful, fear they will have their voices cancelled.

The internet has become a global fishbowl in which anything you wish to say or share is subject to the tyrannical power of the desecrators to silence anyone at any time for any reason.

7.

This awesome power could have never been anticipated by our American founders. The only power that came close was the faraway king against whom they declared a war of independence. Today's American tech oligarchs have unlimited resources and the power to silence anyone or anything. It makes one wonder how to wage a war of independence from Google, Facebook, Twitter, and other social-media giants.

We could speculate that tech titans are under an evil spell and have simply lost track of the truth. But what is more likely is they have simply been captured by the same forces that have been able to transform all other power structures in America: charitable foundations, universities—many of them formerly Christian—media, publishing, unions, corporations, and mainline Protestant Churches.

If you are a Christian or a Jew, you understand the fight of good versus evil. The Old Testament is replete with graphic examples of the depravity of evil and the persecution of the Chosen People. Christians see redemption in suffering and understand that persecution can draw a believer closer to our Creator.

Americans must affirm the reality of evil. They must stop assuming the (alleged) good intentions of those who speak so sweetly in the name of inclusion and care for the oppressed. This mask of deceit must be stripped away to reveal the brute power grab that it is.

The desecrators understand that they must destroy the whole concepts of the family and gender to bring about the chaos to which they are so dedicated. Thus, they use the educational system to poison the minds and hearts of our children, to make them doubt themselves, turn against their parents, their faith, and even their nation.

And what will people of faith do when they finally realize the Left doesn't just want a little more government and a little less Constitution, when they recognize the evil being perpetrated at every level of society? Will the faithful relent or will they defend what keeps diverse people living together in relative harmony?

We offer this book as a blueprint to find the gumption to fight back and to defend the societal order centered on the family which has been so enduring. This moment in history is at a crossroads: the America envisioned by the founders hangs in the balance, as do freedom-loving individuals around the globe.

We can still win the cultural fight, but we have no time to waste.

But mostly, we wrote this book to name the names and to highlight the most grotesque modern forms of a malign effort to take us all down, to desacralize our lives and communities. We have stayed in our homes; we have tried to make friends with those who want to end America and traditional society. None of that worked.

So now we are writing it all down in an attempt to motivate you to join us and to make a last-ditch effort to reconnect with our Maker to see if there is a viable path to defend America. In doing so, we can begin to gain ground against a very real evil that has amassed great public power while we have focused on our daily commitments and responsibilities.

The fight has been joined, but we will not prevail without understanding the extent to which those who wish to take us down have been able to undermine most of what has brought us to where we are today.

We are in a battle on sacred ground. The ground of all that exists is God's love, His sharing of existence through the world He created, and particularly through the human beings who reflect His image and likeness.

Remember that where we fight is sacred ground; thus, it's a conflict about what our lives mean and how we should live.

One hundred years from now, our great-grandchildren will either live in one nation under God or live in a divided nation under the desecrators' idols. Let us reclaim this great country now, so help us God.

CHAPTER I

Talking About Desecrators

1.

This book argues that the desecrators are doing all they can to destroy respect for the Church, America, and the citizen virtues that the founders considered necessary for our nation to grow and flourish.[1]

Yes, we said virtues. It's an old-fashioned word that the founders constantly preached, and it's importance should be repeatedly emphasized. Virtues are the moral habits that spontaneously direct what we feel, think, and do. A courageous person, for example, does not immediately shrink from danger.

In a sense, virtues are more important than principles because virtues are the way principles become ingrained in individual and group character. Virtues ensure that principles will be acted upon. When we address the complicated question of American character, we will be looking for those

---

[1]   Mike Sabo, "The American Founders Knew A Virtuous Republic Requires Virtuous People," *The Federalist*, April 28, 2017, https:// thefederalist.com/2017/04/28/the-american-founders-knew-a-vir tuous-republic-requires-virtuous-people/.

character traits, or virtues, that have become dominant in the fabric of America.

We are not interested in writing clever screeds or adding to the angry condemnations of what we see as necessary to America's recovery of its visionary roots. Neither cleverness nor anger will help to reverse the discouraging trends we will spotlight. We have named the enemy the desecrators because we think it is entirely fair and accurate.

We are writing on the assumption that our arguments will be more effective if their tone is respectful toward those with whom we disagree. We want to equip our readers with arguments, not with hate. This does not mean we will be throwing softballs. On the contrary, we will be as hard-hitting as necessary within the bounds of charity.

2.

People stop listening when they feel dismissed or, at the extreme, hated. We don't hate anyone, because we don't believe anyone should be written off, no matter how destructive they have become to the principles and values that constitute the American character.

Recall Lincoln's second inaugural address in 1865: "With malice toward none, with charity for all, with firmness in the right as God gives us to see the right, let us strive to finish the work we are in, to bind up a nation's wounds, to care for him who shall have borne the battle and for his widow and his orphan, to do all which may achieve a just and lasting peace among ourselves and will all nations."[2]

---

[2]   Abraham Lincoln, "Lincoln's Second Inaugural Address," National Park Service, updated April 18, 2020, https://www.nps.gov/linc

To write with charity and firmness is always a challenge. We anticipate that some readers will open the book hoping for a red-meat harangue against the ideas and leadership we oppose. We began this project with the assumption that there are plenty of those books around and observe they have done little to move the ball down the field—that is, to achieve positive change.

No doubt, what we observe about our nation's problems, and what we propose to help correct them, will offend some people regardless of how we say it. Regarding the possibility of giving offense, we agree with Patrick Henry in his famous speech to the Second Virginia Convention in 1775: "Should I keep back my opinions at such a time, through fear of giving offense, I should consider myself as guilty of treason towards my country, and of an act of disloyalty toward the majesty of heaven, which I revere above all earthly kings."[3]

At this moment in time, our nation is fortunate to have several leading politicians with the fierce and eloquent directness of Patrick Henry. Senators Ted Cruz, Marsha Blackburn, Rand Paul, and Mike Lee immediately come to mind. All hold nothing back whether on the Senate floor or in the media, and all are as smart as and more informed than anyone who tries to bring them down.

The lesson is obvious: it's one thing to be fearless and quite another to be articulate and fully in command of your subject.

/learn/historyculture/lincoln-second-inaugural.htm.

[3] Patrick Henry, "Speech in the Virginia Convention," March 23, 1775, https://www.redlandsusd.net/site/handlers/filedownload.as hx?moduleinstanceid=24801&dataid=32677&FileName=Speech _in_the_Virginia_Convention.pdf.

I had grown up a Presbyterian but became attracted to the evangelical Christianity of a Southern Baptist church while in college. A year after walking the aisle of that church to be baptized, I was elected president of the Southern Baptist Student Union of the University of Texas at Austin. Being a philosophy major at UT caused a problem to some fellow evangelicals on campus; one of whom told me I was "going to hell" if I didn't change my major. During that year as SBSU president, plus the three years I spent at Princeton Theological Seminary and several years as an assistant pastor of a Southern Baptist church in Atlanta, I constantly ran into "fire and brimstone" attitudes towards my philosophical and literary studies and my pursuit of a doctorate.

I was made aware in seminary of the importance of philosophy and other humanistic studies in the Catholic tradition, and gradually I was drawn into the Church for what I regarded as the fullest realization of the Gospel. After my conversion at age thirty-four, I found myself comparing my journeys as a Southern Baptist with being a Catholic. I wanted to share with others my joy in becoming a Catholic but quickly realized that sharing had to be different in tone and style from my Baptist days.

The first invitation I received to speak about my conversion gave me the chance to collect my thoughts about what I called "the rhetoric of apologetics." I think it surprised my audience in San Diego when I said that a Catholic bearing witness did not need to scream, shout, become red in the face, or wave a Bible. It is the Church, I said, that does the converting, not any one person, no matter how articulate or enthusiastic. I know several people, for example, whose road to conversion began when they entered a Catholic cathedral for the first time. I know others who were converted by reading Dante, Flannery O'Connor, or G. K. Chesterton. The Church has such an abundance of truth, beauty, and goodness that you, as a witness, should point it out and then get out of the way.

In this way, a person does not feel like a set of beliefs are being rammed down his or her throat, or pressed upon you to assuage any guilt. Someone has recommended you look this way, toward the Church, and you looked. And like Dante, as he comes into view of the Triune God, you couldn't look away.

—Deal W. Hudson

Chapter 2

Why We Hope

"Although he should kill me, I will trust in him."
—Job 13:15, DRA

1.

W e challenge the widely held notion that America is in inexorable decline. Only by taking the long view through the eyes of faith can we place our present concerns about the future in the context of hope. Hope means that we have confidence that good lies in our future, and this hope is difficult but possible to attain.[1] What is it that makes hope difficult? Saint Paul puts his finger on it in Romans 8:24: "For in this hope we were saved. Now hope that is seen is not hope. For who hopes for what he sees?"

In other words, hope must push beyond the present evidence and trust that God is in our future.

Too often we hear reference to Oswald Spengler's book *The Decline of the West* (1922), a one-size-fits-all explanation of the present age. But Spengler was a man in the grip of atheistic ideas of German philosophers like Nietzsche who

---

[1]   See Thomas Aquinas, *Summa Theologiae*, 2.2. Q 17.1.

no longer viewed human existence as a product of God's creative will. Hope had no place in Spengler's analysis of the West because there was no divine power transcending history to impact or reverse its decline.

When we, as Catholics, speak of retrieving or restoring America, we must have faith that our human efforts will be met by God's blessing. Once again, Saint Paul has just the right words: "Let us hold fast the confession of our hope without wavering, for he who promised is faithful" (Heb 10:23).

Thus, while recognizing America is in a period of decline, we are not implying that decline is some part of the inevitable end of Western civilization or decline of the West. If we believe the faith we confess, then such a pessimistic attitude is anathema.

The life of a Christian is always "on the way." While in this life, we are pilgrims on the way towards the last four things—death, judgment, and eternal happiness or damnation. As the Catholic philosopher Josef Pieper writes, "It would be difficult to conceive of another statement that penetrates as deeply into the innermost core of creaturely existence as does the statement that man finds himself, even until the moment of his death, in the *status viatoris*, in the state of being on the way."[2]

If this world and its temporal powers are all that exist, then there is very good reason for pessimism indeed. Looking back at recorded history, the greatest civilizations have come and gone, not just the Persians, Greeks, Romans, Ottomans, and British, but also the Vikings, Mongols, Mayans, Aztecs, Incas, Mongols, Egyptians, Sumerians, Assyrians, and Mesopotamians.

---

[2]   Josef Pieper, *Faith Hope Love* (San Francisco: Ignatius Press, 1997), loc. 61 of 982, Kindle.

The Hebrews are another of these ancient civilizations, its first stirrings felt in the nineteenth century BC. In spite of the Diaspora and the centuries of persecution, Judaism remains strong, and the nation of Israel has been restored. Our Church grew out of these spiritual roots and has lasted over two thousand years and shows no sign of disappearing. Just the opposite, in fact; its growth in non-Western countries is astounding.[3]

2.

This brings us to the fact that history itself is on the way towards its end. The *Catechism of the Catholic Church* reads: "Creation has its own goodness and proper perfection, but it did not spring forth complete from the hands of the Creator. The universe was created 'in a state of journeying' (*in statu viae*) toward an ultimate perfection yet to be attained, to which God has destined it. We call 'divine providence' the dispositions by which God guides his creation toward this perfection."[4]

Faith, hope, and love are theological virtues, meaning they require the infusion of grace to reside in the human heart and mind. However, hope is the only one of these virtues that cannot be found in a form undergirded only by the unaided human reason and will. Why?

Josef Pieper, commenting on Saint Thomas Aquinas, explains "that we mean that hope is a steadfast turning toward the true fulfillment of man's nature, that is, toward

---

[3]   Elizabeth A. Foster, "How Africa is transforming the Catholic Church," *The Washington Post*, September 9, 2019, https://www.washingtonpost.com/outlook/2019/09/09/how-africa-is-transforming-catholic-church/.

[4]   *Catechism of the Catholic Church*, no. 302.

good, only when it has its source in the reality of grace in man and is directed toward supernatural happiness in God."[5]

Once again, the American understanding of history is entirely different from all of those who pessimistically conclude from the violence of some members of Black Lives Matter and Antifa that America is falling off a cliff and cannot be rescued. If daily life in our nation and others has become depressing and grinding, one should notice that Pieper connects hope to "the enchanting youthfulness of our great saints." True hope is not founded on what is seen and heard in our contemporary world: "It bestows on mankind a 'not yet' that is entirely superior to and distinct from the failing strength of man's natural hope."[6]

As we survey this moment in the history of America and our Church, the element most missing is hope. When everyone becomes focused on narrow temporal means—this candidate, that policy—the long view of history, the conviction that God remains active in history, is forgotten. As G. K. Chesterton said, "hope means having hope when things seem hopeless, or it is no virtue at all."[7]

Hope is not only confidence in the afterlife but an expectation that the future can be better, a greater good, for human life and society. Rather than being grim, angry, and forlorn, those who possess hope exude a youthfulness that springs steps and lights up faces.

---

5   Josef Pieper, *Faith Hope Love* (San Francisco: Ignatius Press, 1997), loc. 66 of 1082, Kindle.

6   Ibid., loc. 73 of 1082, Kindle.

7   G. K. Chesterton, *Heretics*, www.gutenberg.org/files/470/470-h/470-h.htm.

After all, one who believes knows the bottom line—namely, that all of this, the substance of our worries, will one day vanish. Where the world will end is known too, but what we don't know is where we will live in eternity. Accepting this hard reality will alleviate the burden of daily headline despair.

If we do not engage this battle with hope, then we cannot prevail. Hope unites us with Him "for in him all things were created, in heaven and on earth, visible and invisible, whether thrones or dominions or principalities or authorities—all things were created through him and for him" (Col 1:16).

Chapter 3

Shaming in a Toxic Culture

1.

Hope took a severe beating during the four years of the Trump presidency. The constant attacks and false accusations by the media contributed to a toxic culture. Each day, the mainstream media acted more like news-destruction machines; the poison that filled the air was as debilitating as it was depressing.

All the major media outlets melted down into tabloids competing with each other for the most brazen or scary headline. And all of us woke up each morning to another round of nasty charges and accusations against the president.

As the Trump era progressed, it went well beyond sensationalist headlines: they became, in a word, outlandish, not just against Trump, but against all his supporters. They were as racist, uneducated, and irredeemable as they believed the president was.

The same media did not allow any real ability to explain, defend, or, by the end, speak at all. Anger, hostility, and hatred became our daily bread.

The nation, it seemed, was turning inside out—evidence didn't matter and speculative opinion pieces were shared nation-wide as if they were facts. The phrase "fake news" arose against the liars, but the liars just threw it back to the truth-tellers.

The calumnies mounted so high that Twitter felt justified in removing the president's account, and Facebook followed suit. Trump was accused of the very crime the left-wing media was doing hourly—lying.

Twitter and Facebook's action effectively signaled to people in Red America that they were no longer welcome on the major social media news platform. Anyone who supported the president was forced to look elsewhere for honest news or, at least, the other side of the argument.

This led to a brand-new sorting of all platforms and out-lets. Silencing legitimate voices has always occurred but not to this extent. Not only were the polls from the news outlets entirely inaccurate throughout the entire race, almost as if to make it implausible that Trump could win a second term, they then quickly turned when the results were razor tight into defending the outrageous and ahistoric election process.

Before Trump was deemed "canceled," he was constantly shamed. New charges appeared daily: women, marriages, affairs, fat-shaming, pageant-peeping, racist, xenophobic, anti-Semitic, snobbery, dead-beat, bully, embezzler, fraud, fascist, homophobe, white nationalist, business failure. And this was before he even secured the GOP nomination.

Many of the same "journalists" and TV show hosts who attacked Donald Trump for having multiple wives and a onetime playboy lifestyle basically lived their lives in the same manner for which they tried to shame Trump.

2.

Shame is perhaps the best weapon against any person on the political right for this simple reason: conservatives claim to rest their political decisions on a clear set of moral values. That vulnerability can make them easy targets for those who live in glass houses. The left doesn't have quite the same problem because its notion of a moral value is so amorphous—acceptance—that there's little vulnerability to being called a hypocrite.

Those who hold traditional values that can be traced back to Scripture were also raised to accept their failings, be sorry, seek forgiveness, and do better. In the public square, that only works if you are a liberal who "knows in my heart" that he or she did not really commit the wrong under public discussion.

In other words, there is an undeniable double standard.

The kind of viciousness on display is not the acts of Democrats alone. Before the race, a group of Republicans (some of them were actually former Republicans) created the Lincoln Project. Their central aim was to defeat Donald Trump and his Republican allies.

But, get this, they created a list of all those who had "enabled" Trump and sought to bring pressure on employers never to hire them, ever. In other words, this is about more than winning an election; it's about ruining the lives and careers of those with whom they disagree.

Some of this same calumny was directed at those who had worked for the Bush/Cheney Administration. They were called war criminals, with the result that even cabinet secretaries had difficulty finding employment after the second Bush term ended in 2008.

So the problem is not as simple as the difference between Republican and Democrat: it's about persons using their power to destroy those who disagree with them. Forget liberality! Forget human respect!

3.

Of course, if good conservatives can be shamed and put on the defensive so that each time they talk they have to start with a preamble of their sins—which is very hard to detail in a tweet by the way—it becomes clear that this state of shame is the life-in-prison alternative to the cancelation death penalty.

In either case, you will never be able to fully enjoy your rights nor express your gifts, simply because you think cops keep peace, the military keeps American safe, George Washington was the greatest American, and Christopher Columbus was a brave hero of history.

Perhaps one of the best ways to overcome the fear instilled in us by the enemy is to get angry and to recognize the lies being told about you, the injustice of those who want to hurt you and ruin you.

Another way to combat fear is to fight alongside friends and associates, like an army. Veterans of Iwo Jima and D-Day say the buddies all around them kept them moving forward. "I couldn't let them down," they say.

It's hard to fight alone, and it's not necessary. There are literally millions of Americans who want to engage in the battle for our nation's future. We must find a way to stand shoulder-to-shoulder with one another. We need to feel that fierce determination not to let each other, our buddies, down.

After all, it's a battle, just as real as the one fought to give our country its independence. Now we are fighting to keep our nation free, the nation that our founders envisioned.

When liars and fools seek to shame us, we should laugh in their faces. But we should do more: we should expose their ignorance and hatred.

When we fear, we should remember to chart our own course, continue to work together, and not be bullied into submission.

I have personally experienced the Left's use of shaming. Mostly coming from supporting President Trump and other conservatives at the Conservative Political Action Conference (CPAC).

At the annual gathering of CPAC, as many as three hundred speakers opine and thousands of attendees buy tickets and show up. Numerous media forces are in attendance, including a huge number of talk show hosts that form a section called "media row." Hundreds of organizations set up booths in the giant exhibit hall. For the organizer of this massive event, it can be intimidating. If merely one speaker says anything over the line, it gets tossed in your face for years to come. This despite not asking for any preapproved speeches ahead of time.

It is, of course, preposterous for CPAC leadership to be responsible for every word that is spoken during a conference that encourages vigorous debate and is known for fiery rhetoric.

So why do the Left and its allies in the media always begin their coverage with blaming us for something that is said in some room by one speaker who was simply making his or her views public?

It's because shame works on people who have well-formed consciences. I actually do feel partially responsible for what occurs during the unavoidably hectic weekend. I want everyone to be safe and the thousands of students there to feel like the weekend helped arm them to go back to campus and make it through. I want conservatism to put its best ideas forward and for the Left to sweat.

When you invest that much time in an enterprise, you are sensitive to criticism. It affects you when critics do not say it was an impressive event, but that it was filled with racists, haters, and extremists.

—Matt Schlapp

Chapter 4

Let's Make Character King Again

1.

Would anyone who lived through the civil rights conflicts of the '50s and '60s have ever predicted that
one day the "aspects and assumptions" of "whiteness" would
become a subject for display in a national museum?

For many white Americans, the day August 28, 1963,
was a turning point in their racial attitudes. The speech by
Martin Luther King Jr. on the steps of the Lincoln Memorial transformed white confusion and bitterness into a new
understanding of the civil rights movement. King made
clear what his demonstrations had been about: not to pose
a threat to white America but to challenge them to help
African-Americans to fully realize the promise of the American founding—human rights and dignity—to all Americans. "I have a dream that my four children will one day live
in a nation where they will not be judged by the color of
their skin, but by the content of their character."

Throughout the nation, some fairly hardened-hearts nodded in agreement. For those of us who did not grow up

during the segregation era, the major takeaway of America's cruel race history is that since one can't control what race one is born into, it is dehumanizing to shame one because of their race or due to stereotypes about their race. Many bought into the idea that acceptance along racial lines would dissipate our differences and strengthen our national unity. Sadly, we have learned over the course of these decades that in order to achieve greater racial harmony, we have to blunt those who at every step try to exasperate racial divisions.

In the summer of 2020, the National Museum of African American History, part of the Smithsonian, posted a graphic[1] in its "Talking About Race" portal describing fourteen categories of "white dominant culture, or whiteness."

Native Alaskans, it is said, see many variations of what we call *white*, and one website has listed fifty-two variations of the color, from "Abbey White" and "Abstract White" to "Whitest White" and "Whitewash."[2] The contrast between the shades of actual whiteness and the monochromatic whiteness of National Museum of African American History is instructive. One-size-fits-all generalizations of ethnic groups is nothing less than prejudice, no matter who is generalizing or what is being generalized.

The graphic was ultimately taken down,[3] but not before it caused a furor among some and a wake-up call for far more.

---

[1]   "Aspects & Assumptions of Whiteness & White Culture in the United States," National Museum of African American History, https://pbs.twimg.com/media/Ec90PqvXgAc2z16?format=png& name=large.

[2]   Anna Mar, "52 Types of White Color," Simplicable, September 5, 2018, https://simplicable.com/new/white-color.

[3]   Peggy McGlone, "African American museum site removes 'white-

The average person, white or black, had no idea that the academic community had cooked up a racist description of white people. Racism and prejudice, of course, exists wherever judgments are made about individuals based upon a group they belong to, whether their race, color, religion, ethnicity, etc.

This covert attempt to cook up shame on a mass scale—white guilt or any guilt associated with any skin color—is repellent. Those who begin to buy into the museum's account of whiteness will soon discover their supposed "white privilege," meaning their participation in the oppression of African Americans. Of course, if anyone denies this alleged whiteness or privilege, the museum has a diagnosis for that too: it is called "white fragility."[4] According to this, whites make "defensive moves" in the face of racial stress: "The feelings associated with white fragility often derail conversations about race and serve to support white supremacy. While these feelings are natural human reactions, staying stuck in any of them hurts the process of creating a more equitable society. The defensiveness, guilt, or denial gets in the way of addressing the racism experienced by people of color."[5]

Stated another way, if you don't accept the National Museum of African American History's narrative about whiteness, you are in denial and guilty. That is one way, for sure, to inhibit rational dialogue about the issue of racism:

ness' chart after criticism from Trump Jr. and conservative media," The Nation Thailand, July 18, 2020, https://www.nationthailand.com/news/30391542.

4   "Whiteness," National Museum of African American History and Culture, accessed September 28, 2021, https://nmaahc.si.edu/learn/talking-about-race/topics/whiteness.

5   Ibid.

simply label those who disagree as hiding from the truth about themselves. In other words, shaming.

2.

The museum's outline of "whiteness" falls into five categories: "Rugged Individualism," "Family Structure," "Emphasis on Scientific Method," "History," and "Protestant Work Ethic." Is it wrong to acknowledge that people across racial and ethnic communities can see the virtues associated with these concepts? If we can't find common ground in these virtues, then what will unite people who come to this country in an effort to build a better life?"

Such qualities and attitudes are hard to fault, but within the museum's typology, there is an implied critique; namely, why should we "privilege" the nuclear family, Western history, rational thinking, hard work, and self-reliance?

Rugged individualism is somehow stretched into the conclusion "You get what you deserve." The Protestant work ethic repeats a variation on that: "If you didn't meet your goals, you didn't work hard enough." There is, after all, a tragic dimension of life where injustice intervenes to deny persons the fruit of their hard labor. We think people, no matter how individual or hard-working, know life isn't always fair, making the museum a purveyor of silly stereotypes.

Meanwhile, this racial stereotyping is doing damage. An associate dean at Arizona State University, Professor Asao Inoue, published a 358-page book asserting that grading student writing is both racist and a consequence of "white supremacy."[6] Here's an example of the professor's rationale

---

6   Chrissy Clark, "Arizona State Dean: Grading Writing Based On

that determining levels of literacy is racist: "Because all grading and assessment exist within systems that uphold singular, dominant standards that are racist, and White Supremacist when used uniformly." He writes that the very notion of "ranking" is "part of a much longer racist, and White supremacist, tradition in Western intellectual history."[7]

Therefore, educational standards are wrong because the "systems" they exist within are racist, etc.

Let's see: "racist practices" would include spelling words correctly, insisting upon subject-verb agreement, the proper use of pronouns, and writing in complete sentences, all of which Professor Inoue does with great facility. He must have been taught well within the *racist systems* he postulates. Grammatical rules exist to ensure genuine communication between persons in order to avoid misunderstanding and possible conflict. Why throw away a standard that contributes to the common good? Imagine how a child must feel in a writing class where the teacher righteously explains the "white supremacy" of requiring students to spell correctly.

The desecrators do not stop at the use of language. They also want to include what's considered the most precise of practices: mathematics. In October 2019, Seattle public schools issued a new set of learning directives. Questions to be addressed in a math class include "Where does Power and Oppression show up in our math experiences?" and "How is math manipulated to allow inequality and oppression to

---

Quality Is 'Racist,' Promotes 'White Language Supremacy,'" *The Daily Wire*, March 5, 2021, https://www.dailywire.com/news/arizona-state-dean-grading-writing-based-on-quality-is-racist-promotes-white-language-supremacy.

[7]   Ibid.

persist?"[8] Tracy Castro-Gill, the Seattle public school eth-
nic-studies program manager, tried to clarify by saying that
"math is not inherently racist. . . . It's how math is used as a
tool of oppression." It's true such uses are made, but the correct setting to consider such abuses is in a philosophy, logic,
or sociology class, all of which would apply rational analysis
to the use of numeric data.

The introduction to the museum graphic asserts these
attitudes have become "standard practices in the United
States," and we have all internalized aspects of "white culture"—including people of color. Of course, internalization
is a very good thing when it leads to good moral and intellectual habits. Internalization of similar values is precisely what
a society desires if it's to retain a strong unifying identity.

We would like to ask the gurus at the National Museum
of African American History what they would suggest is better than habits such as self-reliance and hard work. Perhaps
more importantly, we would ask what's a better place to raise
children than in a family. As for their critique of "rational
linear thinking," the museum writers employ it quite well.
All of their arguments are based upon the same kind of rational discourse they accuse of "whiteness."

The museum's definition of "whiteness" of the Protestant
work ethic, of course, ignores the work ethic of all the Catholic immigrants from Ireland, Scotland, England, and Europe
who built this nation's infrastructure, escaped poverty, gained

---

8   Elise Takahama, "Is math racist? New course outlines prompt
     conversations about identity, race in Seattle classrooms," Chicago
     Tribune, October 10, 2019, https://www.chicagotribune.com/life
     styles/sns-tns-bc-edu-math-racist-20191010-story.html.

an education, bought a house, and sent the kids to college. Max Weber, in his famous *The Protestant Ethics and the Spirit of Capitalism* (1905), argued that Catholicism slowed down the development of capitalism in the West, but writing in 1905, he did not live to see the rapid ascent of immigrant descendants into the middle class and above.

But, according to the museum, whiteness is guilty of inflicting constant harm against African Americans: "Whiteness (and its accepted normality) also exist as everyday micro-aggressions toward people of color. Acts of micro-aggressions include verbal, nonverbal, and environmental slights, snubs or insults toward nonwhites. Whether intentional or not, these attitudes communicate hostile, derogatory, or harmful messages."[9]

On the subject of micro-aggressions, there is little to say, given that they are entirely subjective. This does not mean they don't happen; it means that anyone's report cannot be scrutinized publicly since the hurt lies within the subject.

The desecrators are very clear about defining the rules of what is appropriate when it comes to race. Even movies that helped change society to be more racially tolerant are now considered off-limits because they are too focused on the white commercial audience (the very audience they wanted to impact). Take the case of the actor Sidney Poitier. Turner Classic Movies recently hired a desecrator, film historian Jacqueline Stewart, to go through the massive film library to identify those films "troublesome or problematic." One of the

---

9   "Whiteness," National Museum of African American History and Culture, accessed September 28, 2021, https://nmaahc.si.edu/learn /talking-about-race/topics/whiteness.

films she wants taken out of circulation is *Guess Who's Coming to Dinner* (1967), starring Sidney Poitier. Directed by the very liberal Stanley Kramer, the film was intended to break down racial barriers by presenting an engaged couple—a white woman and a black man—arriving at the woman's home to meet her white parents, played by Spencer Tracy and Katherine Hepburn. The film caused a sensation and was very well received by critics and the movie-going public.

Stewart expresses appreciation of the career of Poitier, a black actor who succeeded in becoming mainstream in a predominately white film industry, but there's a problem, she says: "there are aspects of his films that are clearly oriented primarily to white audiences. That opens up all kinds of complications for black viewers who felt that he wasn't a representative of the race as a whole."[10]

In other words, Sidney Poitier was too white in his appearance and manner. *The Guardian* quoted a critic in a 2015 column, "How Sidney Poitier paved the way for Barack Obama," saying he was "a white person's fantasy of blackness."[11] Thus, a great actor, a courageous man, now ninety-four years old, is being canceled in the effort to drive a deeper wedge between the races.

Could Denzel Washington be canceled next? Or could even Barack Obama be canceled, who Joe Biden in 2008

---

[10]　Don Surber, "Sidney Poitier, enemy of the people," (blog), March 6, 2021, https://donsurber.blogspot.com/2021/03/sidney-poitier-enemy-of-people.html.

[11]　Sarfraz Manzoor, "How Sidney Poitier paved the way for Barack Obama," *The Guardian*, May 23, 2015, https://www.theguardian.com/film/2015/may/23/sidney-poitier-paved-barack-obama.

called "a mainstream African American who is articulate, bright, and clean?"

To advance theories of "whiteness" is a racist act and should be condemned with the same confidence and ferocity of the nineteenth-century abolitionists.

Chapter 5

Why Trump Supporters Whispered

1.

Once a label is slapped on your forehead—deplorable, racist, homophobic—fear can easily take hold. And fear makes us hide, and whisper, if we speak at all.

One study of the 2016 election revealed that "secret voters" favored Donald Trump over Hillary Clinton by a two-to-one margin (54 percent to 27 percent).[1] These voters were motivated by concern for reputation, being excluded from groups, and avoiding conflict because "it would make my relationships with people I care about hard if they knew I supported Trump."

The reader may recall the phrase "silent majority" that was coined by President Richard Nixon in a televised speech in November 1969.[2] "And so tonight, to you, the silent major-

---

[1]   Rachel I. McDonald et al., "Motivated Secrecy: Politics, Relationships, and Regrets," American Psychological Association, March 8, 2019, http://www.columbia.edu/~ms4992/Pubs/in-press_McDonald-Salerno-Greenaway-Slepian_MotivSci.pdf.

[2]   "President Nixon calls on the 'silent majority,'" History, November 16, 2009, https://www.history.com/this-day-in-history/nixon

ity of my fellow Americans—I ask for your support," said
Nixon. It was a moment when nationwide protests against
the Vietnam War were at their height. In their constant
coverage of the protest, the three major networks—NBC,
CBS, and ABC—began to soften in their support of the
war. Nixon was right about having a silent majority: polling revealed 77 percent of Americans supported his Vietnam policy. But given the change of tone in media coverage
and the gradual shifting of mood against the war, Americans
were muted in their protest against the protests.

This intimidation into silence was repeated with much
greater effect in the 2016 presidential campaign and election. In the *New York Times*, Bret Stephens took the study
of "secret voters" and ran with it in surprising directions.
His tortured take on this academic survey (from Columbia
University) demonstrates how nutty left-wing punditry has
become. Stephens argued that those voters who feared losing friendship, social standing, and reputation were actually
motivated to support Trump because it was shameful: "Forbidden fruit is appealing not because it is fruit, but because
it is forbidden."[3]

In other words, shame and fear helped Trump be elected
president. The more the media rained insults on potential
Trump voters, the more they supported him. Why? The
media had equated voting for Trump with the seductive lure
of the snake in the Garden of Eden.

-calls-on-the-silent-majority.

[3]   Bret Stephens, "Trump's Whisper Network," *The New York Times*,
       February 14, 2020, https://www.nytimes.com/2020/02/14/opin
       ion/trump-voters-2020.html.

Stephens misses the common sense of the matter (common sense being long-gone from journalism). The media's disdain was an additional motivation but not *the* motivation. From the voter's point of view, what Trump promised America was exactly what this country needed after eight years of Obama.

Stephens demonstrated how once again a member of the media can assume a level of influence that replaces all other considerations. Stephens did make the interesting comment that the "whispering networks" that arose among Trump supporters resembled the networks of women avoiding predatory men. Trump voters, he claimed, became "perhaps the biggest whisper network of all"—the secret voters who provided the unforeseen Trump support to win the 2016 election.

2.

The fact that there are such a large number of voters whispering to each other, afraid of being heard, provides a snapshot of a deeply intolerant nation. The original meaning of the word *tolerance* was the social acceptance of people with different opinions, different tastes, and different ways of life. True tolerance made it possible to have a unity among diversity—*E pluribus unum*—in other words, to build a union confident that its citizenry would not make differences turn into divisions in social structures.

The idea of being a "liberal" was once synonymous with being tolerant. People are allowed, and welcomed, to enter an established community even though they are of a different color, religion, or ethnicity. Those liberals of the past often belonged to the Democratic Party and to groups espousing integration, legal and prison reform, and fairness in public education.

Those liberals don't exist anymore except in the conservative ranks. The Democrat liberal no longer tolerates but demands conformity by threatening public shaming. As a result, conservatives have become the new liberals.

Conservatives are not thought police. They do not, for example, demand American citizens believe in "systemic racism." They will happily engage in a conversation or debate about racism in America but won't assume the conclusion ahead of time.

Most of all, Republicans will not apply denigrating labels to people who disagree with them, beyond someone being "too liberal" or "too conservative."

The idea of a liberal education is dying a slow death, though there are notable pockets of resistance at every educational level. At its core, liberal education is based on the idea of learning in freedom (*libertas*) to become free. Education at the hands of the desecrators is indoctrination; it is the opposite of free learning. It is an indoctrination enforced by the fear of shaming and exclusion.

The time for whispering is over. No one evangelizes in a whisper. The idea of the truth about human existence being hidden is itself a desecration.

As an undergraduate at the University of Texas in the late '60s, I had a philosophy professor, Dr. Larry Caroline. He was the campus Marxist who wore sandals and sported long hair and a scruffy dark beard. Though I was a philosophy major, I was a conservative who was growing more and more interested in the evangelical Christian faith. I took his class on modern political philosophy because I was intrigued by his image and reputation on campus.

Dr. Caroline divided the class into small groups who met weekly at someone's home, with everyone sitting on the floor in a circle. At the beginning of each class, he would ask students to share something about their past week. One day, about five weeks into the course, I told the class that I had "become a Christian" and had walked the aisle of a Southern Baptist church. Instantly, there were frowns all around me, but Dr. Caroline smiled, held up his hand, and said, "Good for you. You've made a decision about how to live your life." The frowners stopped frowning; they were as surprised as I was.

But Caroline's remarkable liberalism did not stop there. A few weeks later, I handed in a short paper on J. S. Mill's view of private property. Knowing my professor was a Marxist, I argued hard for the justification of private property. I was expecting some sort of rebuke when he handed it back to me. But no, as Dr. Caroline handed it back, he told the class that my paper was the "best defense of private property he had ever read."

In my memory, that moment represents the best of what traditional liberalism offered: people holding contrary opinions on important subjects could discuss them with civility and even friendship.

—Deal W. Hudson

CHAPTER 6

Our Moment to Shout

1.

As America is desecrated, people of faith and people who still have a patriotic fire must adopt new approaches. We must shout rather than whisper. Often, conservatives are traditionalists, and they wince at the tactics of the Left, of Saul Alinsky, and other communist agitators.

We would argue that tactics in and of themselves should of course be moral, but they do not have to be stale. Armies that fight in old-fashioned ways eventually are slaughtered by military efforts that use surprisingly effective new approaches. The great American resurgence begins with refuting the contention that the anti-socialists are a tiny fraction of America.

Since 2004, registered Republicans have made up around 30 percent of the electorate, while Democrats make up 40 percent.[1] The recent growth of registered Independents

---

[1]   Aaron Blake, "For the first time, there are fewer registered Republicans than independents," *The Washington Post*, February 28, 2020, https://www.washingtonpost.com/politics/2020/02/28/first-time-ever-there-are-fewer-registered-republicans-than-indepen

(29.9 percent in 2020) is significant, making elections more volatile and harder to predict in advance.

Yet Republicans remain nearly 30 percent of registered voters, which is far from being a tiny minority. At the same time, nearly half of Americans in 2020 are members of a church, synagogue, or mosque.[2] However, this percentage has been in decline since 1985 and poses a greater threat to the conservative backbone of America than party registration.[3] Christian voters, whether Catholic, Protestant, or evangelical, are more likely to support a pro-life, pro-family candidate if they are regular church attenders.[4]

For half a century, *Gallup* has charted the breakdown of political philosophies in America: conservative, liberal, moderate. During this time, the two major political parties have become more reliably left and right as Americans continue to sort out of the party of their history and into the party of their beliefs. As of the last round of questions, *Gallup*

---

dents/.

[2]   Jeffrey M. Jones, "U.S. Church Membership Falls Below Majority for First Time," *Gallup*, March 29, 2021, https://news.gallup.com/poll/341963/church-membership-falls-below-majority-first-time.aspx.

[3]   "Politics exists in a flux of ever-changing contingencies. Engaging that flux with the people of faith requires both political savvy and commitment to the first principles that faith provides. The Catholics and Evangelicals of the Religious Right gained political power because they were numerous enough to force the GOP to take a stand on life and the family. Their continued power will depend on both the vitality of their religious communities and the principled translation of that vitality into political action." Deal W. Hudson, *Onward, Christian Soldiers: The Growing Political Power of Catholics and Evangelicals in the United States* (New York: Simon and Schuster, 2008), loc. 5149 of 6255, Kindle.

[4]   Ibid.

charted conservatism as 35 percent of Americans.[5] (Note: this is a higher percentage than GOP membership.) When conservative audiences hear this, they are often surprised. They hear all day long that their values are throwbacks, that kids and young people are woke, and that America is increasingly becoming secular, modernist European, and government loving.

Therefore, conservatives believe there is little hope but to recede. The opposite is true: this is the time to go on the offensive. Now we are warned that conservatives do not make up 60 percent of the country. In other words, conservatives cannot win these battles without attracting Americans who are somewhat uncomfortable with rigid conservative doctrines. Conservatives must understand that if America is to be saved, not everyone will be George Washington or Benjamin Franklin; some will be less molded and even somewhat contrarian. To insist on a harsh uniformity within a coalition is to misunderstand the nature of politics itself, which requires allegiance to each other and not to uniformity.

2.

The vast number of conservatives and people who love America need to be put into context. Sometimes it is easy to forget some of the most basic concepts of Christianity. Jesus recruited the disciples, and even Jesus did not have a perfect HR department. Upon filling the role abandoned by Judas, the remaining apostles voted to select a new twelfth

---

5   Lydia Saad, "Americans' Political Ideology Held Steady in 2020," *Gallup*, January 11, 2021, https://news.gallup.com/poll/328367 /americans-political-ideology-held-steady-2020.aspx.

member, Matthias. In reading this biblical account of the world's first free and fair election, it is important to remember that twelve people, listening to and following God, changed the entire world and built a Church.

The story of the American Revolution is also a story about proper leadership and how an outgunned and dominated group of believers can prevail in the most unlikely of circumstances. Our guess is that people reading this book have experienced lives where success was achieved almost miraculously: in short, they have lived the American Dream. This dream is the combination of the success that occurs when people make mostly good moral choices within a society that rewards those choices despite race, family prominence, religious persuasion, etc. It's imperative that we draw inspiration from God's blessings when we begin to act in accordance with His will for us individually and as a larger group.

History is replete with one decent person standing firmly for what is right and making a historic difference. In 1962, the twenty-nine-year-old James Meredith defied segregation by enrolling at the University of Mississippi.[6] Four years later, Meredith was shot while walking alone as a racial protest from Memphis to Jackson, Mississippi. He put his life on the line and nearly lost it.

Our biggest challenge in America today is that few feel the commitment of a James Meredith. And many believe

---

[6]   Stephen Losey, "58 years ago, James Meredith broke the color barrier at Ole Miss. Here's how the Air Force and Army shaped that battle," *Army Times*, October 1, 2020, https://www.armyt imes.com/news/your-air-force/2020/10/01/58-years-ago-james -meredith-broke-the-color-barrier-at-ole-miss-heres-how-the-air -force-and-army-shaped-that-battle/.

we have lost all the young voters, the funding, and the argument. But this is propaganda unleashed by the Left's desire to discourage us from trying to revive America and the cause of freedom.

Politicians in America can learn lessons. Most desire two things: to win their next election and to become more powerful. Even more of them want to achieve these goals without having to dirty themselves by championing causes that will divide constituencies and make them vulnerable to their own imperfections.

If a politician has entered into the "devil's bargain" of only advocating for non-controversial policy goals like bipartisanship, providing help for those in need, working with global partners, providing more funds for public schools and communities, while only giving lip service to more crucial moral questions during moments of proximity to die-hard supporters, then that politician is like a dog used to getting on the furniture: spoiled and untrainable.

What if politicians went back to fearing taking positions that alienated Catholics and other people of faith? What if politicians had to stand up for the values that help young men start families, help those families prosper, and rebuild the institutions that make society strong? Over time, we were made to feel small and to be discouraged. During this time, too many conservative Republicans and almost every Democrat politician basically told us that our positions were just not relevant in a modern context. Most of us accepted that fact. Therefore, we are also to blame for supporting those politicians who told us abortion was too controversial to discuss and who told us to sit by and do little while new legislation made us complicit in the act of killing the unborn.

The beginning of the Biden administration has unleashed a torrent of morally indefensible policies, so many that it is difficult to even be knowledgeable of them all. This is being done because the left corruptly attained power and now senses how discouraged we must be. As Americans determine how they will respond to the socialist economic policies and fascist cultural policies set upon society, the Republican Party will need to decide its course.

The bigger responsibility and challenge for the party and leaders of the conservative cause is to fight much more aggressively and extensively to defend what we have left to save. This will require a new generation of bold and aggressive leaders who are not parties to the compromises of the previous generations. It will require grassroots leaders and support from public officials from across the country. But it will most definitely require a new brand of politician.

More and more people at the grassroots level are challenging their elected officials on school boards, city councils, state legislatures, and beyond, as the wipeout of the radicalized democratic candidates in the 2021 elections showed, especially in the blue state of Virginia. They have begun to shout, but their voices needs to be amplified by millions.

The story of the 2020 election deserves an accurate version, and one day it will be told. Listening to President Trump at the White House at 2:00 a.m., it was so obvious what had happened. I told White House Chief of Staff Mark Meadows, who was standing near us during the remarks, that Mercy and I were ready to hit one of the disputed states.

Thanks to Ambassador Ric Grenell, I was added to the Nevada Team and witnessed wrongdoing like I had never seen in politics. It was repulsive and blatant illegal behavior.

I talked with President Trump throughout this process. His mind picked up every detail and every category of illegal ballot. He knew a great wrong had occurred, and despite the incompetence of too many from his campaign and the RNC, especially on Election Day Activities Teams run by his re-election lawyers, President Trump wanted to fight the wrongdoing.

He was always willing to fight. Sometimes he fights too hard and for too long. He has no quit. President Trump fought well beyond the comfort level of most DC Republicans. He fought despite irregular legal advice and talent. He fought like anyone would to save a job, a company, or a country.

In the end, Donald Trump lost twice. He lost the election and then he lost his voice. At first, Twitter permanently canceled him, and Facebook and others followed suit. Trump was put in the digital gallows for having the audacity to demand that a national election follow the law on balloting.

Most believe his placement in the digital gulag was due to his alleged complicity with the unruly violent protests in and around the Capitol building on January 6. This charge is of course unproven, particularly the despicable charge that the president had directly encouraged violence, but it also was just an excuse to do what they always intended to do to President Trump: kick him from the national political stage.

Republican presidents truly fade away. It is what they generally tend to do. They do not actively engage in rough and tumble politics after their time is done. It is a graceful way to end a career from a bygone era.

Democrats never stop politicking, fundraising, or self-promoting. It is just what they do.

Donald Trump had one final way to upset the way things usually work, and that was to be the most aggressive GOP/conservative/America First voice from outside the White House. It was obvious as he fought the voting catastrophe that he would never go away quietly.

So they had to silence his voice and the voices of those who support him.

—Matt Schlapp

CHAPTER 7

Politicians Are Not Saints, and Neither Are We

1.

Nowadays, when you speak up for traditional views of moral values, you look around for the frowning faces, not for the possibility that someone will engage your view in a calm, rational way. You look closely at the faces looking for signs or approval or disapproval—in short, you become reflexively paranoid.

How do most people deal with fear? They retreat. They stop speaking out. They try to reverse their shamed image. When that happens, the shamers have won; they have destroyed the enemy—that is us, you and me.

And when a conservative is seen in any way to be less than perfect, then the public humiliation begins. The great irony is that even though we are made in the image and likeness of God, each of us falls short. The charge that a Republican or a conservative is a hypocrite is just too delicious for the Left.

After all, there is a stereotype that every Republican tries to look and act perfect, with carefully choreographed public personas. It is an irresistible cheap shot that goes something like this: "He calls himself a Christian, so he is a hypocrite when . . ." Of course, Republicans and conservatives are perfect examples of some of the least perfect people imaginable.

In fact, it is not their individual holiness that makes them politically powerful but their ideas which still resonate with most Americans, and certainly Americans in most of our states.

But far too often Christian voters, who hold traditional values, give in to the instinct to retreat, like an animal who suddenly flees a predator. But we are not merely animals, we are human beings gifted with an intellect and free will.

In other words, we may feel the urge to run, but we can catch ourselves and consider other options.

2.

President Trump did not run away; in fact, he didn't bat an eye. He taught us all a valuable lesson—to accept the fact that we have all made mistakes and there is no use in dwelling on those mistakes, especially when the hypocritical media is trying to ruin you by making those mistakes disqualifying.

The more you focus on your shortcomings with public self-flagellation, the more you feed the media attention and send a message to your supporters that you can be politically neutered by public shaming.

Instead, Trump shrugged his shoulders—and often laughed. He acknowledged his life as a private citizen, stood his ground, and attacked the hypocrisy of the media. Brilliant!

Rather than apologizing, he reminded voters what he would do as president. No one in any political science class or any campaign ever suggest this as a viable strategy.

It was audacious and incredibly effective. And there was collective exhalation from many Republicans and conservatives, as if they could finally stop pretending and admit they would like to hang out behind the velvet rope with the rich and famous. Or that some of them might also like to have an apartment in the sky filled with gold furniture and a beautiful wife. In other words, Trump might have his flaws, but these voters appreciated a candidate who told them forthrightly what he would do if elected president. The truth is that for all those decades when many Republicans ran around pretending to be nearly perfect, no one was really buying it.

Voters know that life is messier than any campaign photo. Everyone has challenges in life, and each one of us has had triumphs and failings. Christians are taught that they stumble daily, and they should be sorry and aware of those constant failings.

Christians have long been taught the traditional virtues of courage and prudence. Courage keeps you in pursuit of what is good in spite of danger. Prudence considers all the relevant factors needed to make a wise decision.

Since both courage and prudence are habits, also called virtues, we are usually not aware of being courageous and prudent—we just act that way if we have those virtues. But sometimes we are hit with a label so potentially damaging that we are momentarily dazed.

3.

The most toxic tactic associated with shaming is the smear of racism. There is no way to escape its putrid stink.

There was a time when racism was used to call out segregation and Jim Crow. Today, the charge of racism is mostly used to silence conservatives, not to actually call out bad behavior.

The tragic part is that millions of Americans growing up before 1960 who shed old hateful attitudes on race are facing a shaming based on the color of their skin, not what they believe or how they act. The charges of systemic racism being made have come as a surprise to those who experienced segregation.

Christians don't believe that skin color determines destiny. They believe that original sin is the only hereditary sin. It is the sin common to all human beings. The meaning of human dignity taught in Catholic social teaching makes no mention of ethnicity or skin color precisely for the reason that the concept of inherent dignity is common to all individuals regardless of demographic differences.

In fact, the Church reverses the view on human dignity from having anything to do with any earthly factor: "The dignity of the human person is rooted in his creation in the image and likeness of God."[1] For this reason, Thomas Jefferson called certain basic human rights "unalienable," meaning they cannot be removed by any political community. Dignity belongs to persons by their very nature, as created by God Who shared with them in His "image and likeness."

---

[1]   *Catechism of the Catholic Church*, no. 1700.

Human dignity means persons possess the freedom to direct their lives and grow in character. The decisions you make in your life, including to practice tolerance and acceptance of others, help create your character. As the *Catechism* continues, "By his deliberate actions, the human person does, or does not, conform to the good promised by God and attested by moral conscience."[2]

In other words, ethnicity does not determine who we are or what we become. Christians are taught that in small acts of kindness, the corresponding growth in an admirable character can impact others who observe and create a system of virtuous behavior.

The role of the individual and his conscience, formed by knowledge and spiritual guidance, can actually change his community and his community can in turn change a country. "With the help of grace they grow in virtue, avoid sin, and if they sin they entrust themselves as did the prodigal son to the mercy of our Father in heaven. In this way they attain to the perfection of charity."[3]

When you engage the cultural and political battle, you should expect the desecrators to use your past against you. But do not flinch. It's spiritual warfare and must be seen as a struggle you must engage.

One of the reasons I admired my grandfather was because he always taught me that it was proper to be racially tolerant. He adored Abraham Lincoln and flew his American flag every day I can remember. If he voted

---

[2]   Ibid.
[3]   Ibid.

Republican, it was because it stood for the Union and for the rights of everyone despite their race.

I always believed my grandfather understood the little guy because he had been an impoverished son of an Irish immigrant with deep roots in the North and the South. He saw the racism and violence of his brother, and he knew instinctively it was wrong. But according to the racialists of today's cancel culture, my grandfather, who eventually became a self-taught successful banking executive in Manhattan, was just another white man exploiting the benefits of an evil structure of racism and hate.

These ideas seem so quaint today. I was raised to believe that you fought racism each and every time you walked away from an inappropriate joke or refused to mock the person struggling to speak English. You embraced a true American idea of equal protection when you hired people on abilities and not cultural experience.

—Matt Schlapp

CHAPTER 8

Rejecting the "New Narrative"

1.

The desecrators like to talk about their "new narrative" of American history. The term *narrative* is aptly chosen since it's applied primarily to fiction, not to historical fact. If all of history is a fictional narrative, then the truth is easily molded into whatever shape you choose.

For the purveyors of the new narrative, a fabricated history which teaches that America's history is the history of the evils of slavery and oppression and thus with a more accurate American founding of 1619 rather than 1776, the individual cannot make any moral impact.

A product of the *New York Times*, the "1619 Project" seeks to redefine the American founding in terms of racism and slavery, specifically the arrival of slaves in the colonies at Jamestown. Its director, Nikole Hannah-Jones, admitted, however, "the project is not a history but a fight to control the national narrative."[1] The adoption of the 1619 Project in

---

[1]   Tyler O'Neil, "1619 Project Founder Admits It's 'Not a History,' But a Fight to 'Control the National Narrative,'" *PJ Media*, July

many of the nation's public schools did not come with the warning label "This is not history."

The upshot of the 1619 Project is this: American society and its economic system was started in such a corrupt way and is so irredeemable that it can only be rectified by mass reeducation or a takeover by woke activists. In other words, a new reconstruction.

Today, you will be called a racist by the Left not for actually being racist but for failing to follow the politically acceptable script and mouth the words and phrases that provide evidence that you are a member of "woke" America: Yes, there is "systemic racism," and yes, all whites suffer from "white privilege."

The most tragic part about this effort is that it has nothing to do with cleansing our society of the real evils of racism and bigotry but is instead an indictment against the alleged "white power structure" of a country founded in evil. That's the narrative.

This type of shaming is a cancer. It shames all those who will not use the exact words dictated by radical groups in pressure campaigns aimed at media and corporations. These campaigns are meant not to find healing but to destroy America's founding and replace it with a new country subject to despotic demands.

Fortunately, the 1619 Project is beginning to lose its credibility. Nikole Hannah-Jones was denied tenure teaching journalism at the University of North Carolina and had

29, 2020, https://pjmedia.com/culture/tyler-o-neil/2020/07/29 /1619-project-founder-admits-its-not-a-history-but-a-fight-to-co ntrol-the-national-narrative-n724944.

to settle for a five-year contract.[2] It's rare for a university board of trustees to not approve a tenure recommendation, but in this case, the trustees exerted their responsibility in a way few boards ever do. The UNC faculty predictably wept and wailed, invoking claims of "academic freedom," even as Hannah-Jones's ideas are bogus. A disgruntled faculty eventually bullied the board into offering her tenure, but Jones declined the offer at the University of North Carolina and is now the Knight Chair at Howard University.

2.

If these words in this chapter had been typed a decade ago, they would have seemed paranoid. But after years of violent riots, with unrelenting attacks on our nation's history and her statues, the destruction of our creeds and her churches, and the attacks on the foundational building blocks of all successful societies, the family, these words are not paranoid; they reflect reality.

No law or politician can prevent the tactic of canceling culture. It will be up to each one of us, and we have to work together. Our American moment arrives when we refuse to wear their shame, while being genuinely contrite for what we have done wrong, including full restitution for those we have harmed. We can be humble and contrite without accepting the shame from outsiders who attack not to improve but to bring us down. Reject their shame, which is aimed at putting conservatives on the defense. Shrug it off and stand up

---

2   Katie Robertson, "Nikole Hannah-Jones Denied Tenure at University of North Carolina," *The New York Times*, May 19, 2021, https://www.nytimes.com/2021/05/19/business/media/nikole-hannah-jones-unc.html.

with confidence that America is a good country brimming with millions of decent people.

The country is not perfect; in fact, it allows for the execution of millions of unborn babies each year, but it is a force for good and is the envy of freedom-loving people everywhere.

If we can avoid their shame, then we can cleanse ourselves from their desire to make everyone who loves America and enjoys her bounties a "racist." Even realizing that our personal actions can never rid us of this change should be enough for us to focus on ridding our country of personal racism. And if we can demystify the slur that most Americans are racist, we can defang cancel culture. But this task will require the best of us. If we deny history, we deny the incarnation of Christ and His gift of the Church. History is not an abstraction about which we can be nonchalant; history is the repository of what we believe.

I have been shamed, but I deserved it. In 2004, a moral mistake I made in 1994 was reported by the media. At the time, I was the head of Catholic Outreach for the RNC and host of a weekly "Catholic" call with the Office of Public Liaison in the White House. This was a few months before the 2004 presidential election, but the story made no difference to the outcome: President George W. Bush was elected with the largest number of Catholic votes that any Republican had received in decades.

In the 2000 election, I had led an effort that increased Catholic support for the GOP nominee by 14 percent.

When Karl Rove asked me to head Catholic Outreach, I told him my only conditions were two: the choice of vice president should be pro-life and I would be allowed to voice disagreement with the White House if I thought Catholic teaching was being broken. Rove agreed, and the four years I spent working with the White House were happy ones.

As I told Karl when he asked me to help the campaign, "The only politics I know is Aristotle's *Politics*." My naïveté caught up with me when I became what is known as a "public person." When you become a public person, especially in politics, you become a target for the press who want to discredit you and what you represent. I ended up resigning my posts as director of Catholic Outreach and editor of *Crisis Magazine*, though I remained the publisher and fund raiser.

Only those who have been publicly shamed know how crushing it is. I made it through for three reasons: my family and my true friends continued to love and support me, my faith in God's grace kept me from giving in to the darkness, and Father Benedict Groeschel, CFR, who kept telling me to get over it. "After all," he said, "that's not the only sin you ever committed." It was during the retreats with Father Groeschel that I came to accept the new reality that shame had cast over my life and to forgive myself for bringing it on. Father made it clear, "Get that scarlet A off your head." And I did.

—Deal W. Hudson

CHAPTER 9

Knowing Donald Trump

1.

The life of an ex-president is replete with corporate boards, six-figure speaking fees, unrestricted gifts from donors, and lucrative opportunities for his family. Former presidents can "refill the coffers" and focus only on the policy issues that matter to them.

Republican former presidents are usually so embittered by their treatment by the DC media that they run from politics, seldom to be heard from again until the next GOP convention.

Democrats have not exited the stage so completely. Jimmy Carter constantly opined on public policy through the Carter Center, and the Clintons and Obamas view their roles as formers to lead public discourse from their lofty perches while getting down with the jet set, Hollywood, and corporate America. No ex-president enjoyed as big a lifestyle boost as did Barack Obama, who left the White House picking up enough multi-million-dollar homes to risk forgetting how many.

Those of us who are conservatives respect financial success, especially by those who outcompeted others or brought an interesting product or service to market. As for the architects of socialist policies like the Green New Deal, however, which pushes carbon taxes based on dishonesty about our ability to control the weather in the future, the hypocrisy of them owning massive homes and flying on private jets is more than a bit much.

One of the best things about Donald Trump is that he not only took a two-by-four to the news media and to the establishment but he also threatened the whole model of a post-presidency president.

When I first was invited to meet with Donald Trump in 2015, he was still considering a run for the presidency. Like most of my generation, Donald Trump was a constant name in the news on topics ranging from business to glamour and fame. We read about his staggering wealth, his failures, and his rambunctious romantic life. His books showed up under the Christmas tree, his face in movie cameos, and he would be reliably on-message on various talk shows talking about the stupid thinking of political deal-making.

As a very young child, I remember him appearing on the Phil Donahue Show and later on Oprah Winfrey's show. His family was fascinating, and his first marriage seemed to capture the 1980s goal of finding a spouse who you could partner with at home and on the job.

2.

When I was invited to a meeting with Mr. Trump, all these television memories came rushing back. My parents were born in New York City, and my grandfather, Thomas Spencer Sites, had been a successful banker. During those years, my grandfather had a professional relationship with the Trump organization as he for a time headed up a mortgage division.

Dan Schneider, the top staffer at the American Conservative Union, and I prepared for the meeting in the lobby of Trump Tower and wondered what this interaction was going to be like. We were met in the lobby and taken up in the sky to where we were met by Mr. Trump's always cool and kind secretary, Rhona Graff. The decorating had not changed much in twenty years except that there was more of it: lots of brass and flash with gifts piled on the floor and sports memorabilia everywhere.

Trump sat behind his desk in shirt sleeves and a tie. He was energetic, quick to stand up, and a fountain of information. I immediately felt comfortable and liked him. We were not the same, but I just enjoyed the way he talked and how unfiltered he was. And, of course, I was appreciative to earn the respect of a generous amount of time.

The first thing you realize about Donald Trump is no matter what you want to talk with him about, he has something he wants to talk to you about. I had shown up to see about getting long-term financial support from him for the ACU. Trump had other plans. His goal was to pick my brain on politics and to make me aware that he was seriously considering running for president.

We tried to talk about our project, with Dan Schneider and me passing the ball to each other when Mr. Trump would take a respite. There was another board member with us who had his own agenda. He wanted to enlist Donald

Trump to support Jeb Bush's presidential campaign. When Trump realized this, he had a quick and brutal retort: "He's a loser."

As I made one more attempt to get back to my agenda, Mr. Trump stood up and said that we should resume our conversation in the lobby. He threw on his suit jacket and led us to the Trump Tower lobby where he held court like only he can, taking photos and hamming it up. He generously opened up the cabinets to his merchandise and started handing it to each of us: sunglasses, cologne, ties, and cuff links. As bags were filled, I was standing back, taking nothing. Mr. Trump walked over to me and asked why I was not receiving a bag of goodies. I told him, "I didn't come here to have you give me ties."

Trump interrupted me nicely and whispered, "I know why you are here, and I will call you to discuss what you want." During all the time in his office, Trump figured out everyone's angle. He knew that I was the incoming chairman who wanted his support. He knew the current chairman would never be gauche enough to ask for help and would settle for some cuff links and a photo, which he took and posted on Twitter.

3.

True to his word, Trump called me within a week or so while I was at our farm in the Virginia mountains not far from his winery. When Mr. Trump discovered where I was, he gave me the whole back story on his Virginia golf club and the deal he got on the winery. Being Donald Trump means nothing is boring. He also made it clear during the call that he was serious about running. He never asked me to join his effort, but over the next few months, we had more conversations.

I realized after this that Trump was wickedly shrewd, could read a room, and loved dishing with people. He told wildly entertaining stories. I always wished I had taped the conversations, not to hurt him like too many others have, but to remember the details of his vivid accounts and to be able to demonstrate to people how real he was.

Having never worked for Trump, unlike my wife, Mercy, I probably was shielded from some of the tougher sides of his personality. He did not demand a lot from me. In fact, we never had a direct conversation about what each could do for the other. It just started to happen, as it was clear we were on the same side. As direct as Trump is, he also understands that a part of life is determined by how people either help or hurt you, especially those who claim to be a friend or ally.

I remember Mr. Trump asking me in another meeting if folks in DC thought he was serious about running. I told him that they all thought he was hyping his net worth and that I heard constantly from politicians and consultants that Trump "would never file." This meant that the insiders believed Trump would never file a financial disclosure statement with the Federal Election Commission, which is a mandatory step toward a declaration of candidacy for federal office. These filings give the public its first glimpse into a candidate's financial status. Mr. Trump told me he was going to file and that these people in DC were wrong about his net worth: It's $9 billion. It's all done. I can have the lawyers cart it in here; it's $9 billion! Why would they think I'm not filing?"

I told him that when he filed, everyone in DC would begin to realize that Donald Trump was not just talking; he was serious.

4.

As the early Trump team began to plan for the race, my career had become quite varied. More and more I found myself a guest on political news shows. I started to play a larger role as a former Bush official who was also not a member of Never Trump.

In fact, when the creator of the now-infamous Never Trump *National Review* issue called to ask me to contribute, I was quick to say hell no, from a studio chair in a CNN studio right before the cameras went live. Why were we signing up to say we would rather have another President Clinton instead of an outsider who had told me to my face on multiple occasions that he would push on the conservative policies we had discussed?

The most astonishing take away from my interactions with Donald Trump was that he never acted like a typical presidential candidate. I have been a party to hundreds of "sit downs" with candidates. They are practiced at the ten-minute pitch with answers and a ten-point plan for every hot topic. They pitch; you listen. They sometimes ask for your support at the end, and other times they are perfectly interrupted by staff saying it was time to drive to the next meeting. I have participated in so many of these I have given in to the banality of it all.

Trump was completely different. There were no ten-point plans. Before the first debate in Cleveland, I called him inviting him to our ACU after-party at the House of Blues. We had a great conversation, and I urged him to at least write a two pager on his views on cutting taxes. Trump responded, "Matt, no one reads these things, and they don't even give you enough time to go into details." He also demurred on coming to the event with a very candid reply, "You know, Matt, I've never done a debate. If I do badly, I'm not gonna want to go to a party." He was of course right, and his performance was so unstereotypical. It appeared he was either going to immediately bomb out or skyrocket to the top. We know the path he took.

But the most shocking thing that Donald Trump did was ask loads of questions. He had an insatiable desire to figure out what DC Republicans were thinking when they made such obvious blunders. He wanted to know what made conservatives tick. He listened to my answers and asked tough follow-up questions. He never really made a pitch, but he reiterated his now-familiar themes. He was honest about perceived weaknesses and was clearly pleased that his kids had reached an age where they could take care of the business and be ready for the fight.

5.

I can remember the exact place I was sitting at the NBC DC Bureau on Capitol Hill when I was asked my first question about the newly announced presidential candidate, Donald Trump, and if I supported his "racism," which the reporter said had been exhibited by him calling all Mexican immigrants "rapists" and "drug dealers." I remember having a quiet moment which lasted a split-second but felt like five minutes, and I was given an option. Donald Trump did not call all Mexican immigrants rapists or drug dealers, but in his shorthand language, he was mocking a system that allowed illegal immigrants into our country despite knowing nothing about their background. Trump's conclusion was the opening salvo: a completely new orientation in how a Republican candidly spoke about some of the problems with illegal immigration.

As a former White House political director for President George W. Bush, married to a first-generation Cuban American, I was uncomfortable embracing the full coarseness of Trump's language. But I also knew that he had a very legitimate point that was not about race but about jealously protecting our country from a chaotic immigration system based on sentiment and not on what was best for America. From that first answer, I jumped on the Trump roller coaster. Some days I worried about where it would go, other days I screamed in sheer delight at his unbridled push for policies we had advocated for decades. Five years later, I still cannot believe the roller coaster ended so quickly.

As the reelection campaign was coming to an end, my wife had encouraged me to spend more days on the campaign trail for President Trump and other GOP candidates. I spent days on the Trump bus. I made lifelong friends and met MAGA America. I loved it. I loved them. It felt good to make a difference. We really thought we could win.

From there, Mercy and I spent election day at the White House, both of us arriving in DC directly from the road. We were exhausted but hopeful.

—Matt Schlapp

CHAPTER 10

Be Not Afraid!

1.

We have already discussed the central importance of hope. Hope, of course, drives out fear. Do you remember when Pope John Paul II, now a saint, said, "Be not afraid"? The first time he said it was in Saint Peter's Square on October 22, 1978, a challenge that he repeated throughout his pontificate. His challenge was heard by all people of faith who were determined to defend the unborn and family life. But no one finds it easy to carry out.

Years later, in his book *Crossing the Threshold of Hope*, Pope John Paul II wrote about the origin of that phrase and its meaning:

> The exhortation "Be not afraid!" should be interpreted as having a very broad meaning. In a certain sense it was an exhortation addressed to all people, an exhortation to conquer fear in the present world situation. . . . Why should we have no fear? Because man has been redeemed by God. When pronouncing these words in St. Peter's Square, I already knew that my

first encyclical and my entire papacy would be tied to the truth of the Redemption. In the Redemption we find the most profound basis for the words "Be not afraid!": "For God so loved the world that he gave his only Son" (cf. Jn 3:16).[1]

The pope, who is now *Saint* John Paul II, understood how often fear arises in persons around the world—in his time, over two billion people were ruled by communist regimes, and many remain so. The populations of Mexico and Central and South America are subjected to the violence of drug lords. The countries of the Middle East remain a tinder box with ongoing conflicts in Afghanistan, Iraq, and Israel's occupied territories. Parts of Africa still suffer from genocidal tribal warfare and Christian persecution by Muslim warlords. Saint John Paul II himself had lived through two despotisms, the Nazis and the Soviets.

But the larger meaning of "Be not afraid" was a message to every Christian to not fear speaking the truth about God and His creation, about Adam and Eve, the Fall, the Ten Commandments, the Incarnation, and Resurrection. The Holy Father was well aware that the Church's moral teaching about gender, sexuality, and marriage was under constant attack to the extent that believers had become hesitant to speak up in its defense. "Do not be afraid" means never hesitate to be a witness in what you say and what you do.

Yet, we all know the human instinct to self-preservation is strong. Nothing is more natural than to save yourself in

---

[1]   John Paul II, *Crossing the Threshold of Hope* (New York: Alfred Knopf, 1995).

the face of danger. But Saint John Paul challenged us to transform culture and society and to proclaim the Gospel, its teaching, and its call to salvation. Recall in the Gospel of Matthew when Jesus said of those who went out to see John the Baptist, "What did you go out into the wilderness to behold? A reed shaken by the wind?" (11:7). From the very beginning, the history of the Church has produced martyrs—those who did not shake in the wind, those who were not afraid.

2.

Our nation would not exist without such men and women willing to put their lives on the line. At 11:00 p.m. on Christmas Day 1777, General Washington ordered his 5,400 soldiers to cross the nearly-frozen Delaware River in the middle of the night.[2] They were already suffering from lack of food and clothing in sub-zero weather, and they had been in retreat from a series of defeats in New York and New Jersey. The newly born United States was losing the war and on the verge of becoming a British colony again.

Washington knew that if he waited for the British to converge and attack, the war would be over. So he attacked against the advice of his officers, and his men followed, some with only cloth binding over their feet. The resulting victories in Trenton and Princeton changed the outcome of the war and the nation. Without the courage of Washington and his troops over nine days, the nation would have been lost.

---

[2]   "George Washington crosses the Delaware," History, November 12, 2009, https://www.history.com/this-day-in-history/washington-crosses-the-delaware.

The fight to take back the voice of our nation will rely on men and women who will take the risk of martyrdom. There are martyrs who die, of course, but some of those who today fight the advance of the desecrators, with their tactics of shaming and cancel culture, will suffer in ways that crush their lives. Among those who have been canceled is a list of celebrities, most of whom are already wealthy, such as the author of the Harry Potter series, J. K. Rowling, who questioned the politics of gender identity.

Far more important are those who lost their livelihood and their reputation in the community. One teacher in Michigan was fired for pointing out that "Trump is our president" on his social media and supporting his view that schools should reopen.[3] He was brought before a closed-door meeting and told by the principal to resign or be fired. Variations of this story are being told almost on a daily basis as both parents and teachers protest the indoctrination of the "new narrative."

When we look at all the men and women who have sacrificed all for our free nation, and continue to sacrifice, it must quiet our fears about being publicly shamed. Part of the reason we are writing this book is to help others understand that this push by the desecrators to shame us has actually caused many conservative Americans to remain silent as their country is being depicted as racist, hypocritical, and evil.

---

[3]   Chrissy Clark, "Michigan School Fires Popular Teacher For Saying 'Trump Is Our President,'" *The Washington Free Beacon*, July 21, 2020, https://freebeacon.com/campus/mi-school-fires-popular-teacher-for-saying-trump-is-our-president/.

We must all stop looking around with concern for what other people think of us; to "be not afraid" requires total indifference to those who would use your fear to silence you.

When Mercy and I campaigned across America last year, the consequences of left-wing shaming were obvious and tragic. Mercy and I experienced countless examples of getting off a plane or a bus and talking to voters, most of them for our candidate. Campaigning can be surprisingly intimate as people you just met tell you their fears and their dreams and sometimes get emotional.

I remember being outside a gun shop in Cleveland, and the patrons were a bit less friendly, and I assumed it was because Cuyahoga County, the county of my birth, is very blue. But I talked to a few of the patrons who saw the Trump bus, and one man walked up to me. He said he was not a Republican, but he would vote for Trump. I looked at the man, a smoker, wearing a ball cap and a workingman wardrobe. He did not make much eye contact, and he offered no fluffy compliments. I will never forget what he said as he looked in the distance: "I will vote for Trump because the Democrats think folks like me are worse than scum."

His answer struck me. I felt unworthy of asking a follow-up question. He was encapsulating a key reason why millions of working people were abandoning their previous political posture to vote for President Trump. But one thing was obvious: shame. He knew they looked down at him, at his use of tobacco or his enthusiasm for guns, and maybe because he was a Midwestern white guy who believed it should not be confusing to know which bathroom a man used.

—Matt Schlapp

CHAPTER 11

The Trojan Horse of Social Media

1.

In the midst of the unprecedented political warfare, we are faced with several factors that force us to think more deeply and with more care. One factor is the use of social media—the most cruel and effective vehicle to shame and eventually publicly destroy.

We call it a Trojan horse because the arrival of Google, Facebook, Twitter, Instagram, etc. appeared to be a gift that would encourage greater communication and the building of community. It seemed to be a free-market way to guarantee our ability to offer commentary around the dominant leftist corporate media. Heavens, was that wrong. This gift brought with it some very destructive forces, not unlike the Greek soldiers who snuck in to sack and burn Troy.

How should we respond to an attack in the virtual reality of the internet? Respond in kind, angrily and accusatorily? Ignore it? Or kindly with "I beg to differ?" Perhaps a logical and factual argument? A too-quick Twitter finger can be costly.

Another factor is that people are being seriously harmed by shaming. Jobs have been lost. Businesses hurt or ruined. Reputations destroyed. Families broken apart. It does give one pause before joining the battle of ideas and facts. But without fighting back, without resistance, nothing will change. This is a unique moment in history. Without an all-out effort to stop the lies that are destroying our nation, its history, and values, there may not be another chance. The damage will have become too embedded in our culture.

What was once considered outright nonsense—such as the assertion that the United States was founded to protect slavery—will be considered "common sense." But it is not consensus upon which this nation was founded. What is generally accepted in society will change if there is an all-out effort by elites to change culture over time. To the Southerners of colonial America, for example, the right to own slaves was a matter of common sense. It took a long time, after years of a bloody war, for that immoral assertion to change.

But that nonsense change is already in the works when indoctrinations such as the 1619 Project are being taught in thousands of public and private schools. The 1619 and critical race theory efforts have resulted in a grassroots political revolt by parents in racially charged big cities and small town America. Millions of parents could not believe that this hate had become formalized in their children's schools. And where are the social media oligarchs in this fight to protect patriotic values? Predictably, they are leading the charge to indoctrinate our children and silence and threaten parents online.

We are in the midst of a battle of ideas. The differences could not be clearer, as we have already described. The reader might remember that revolutions are the project of ideas most of all. Certainly, America was the product of the ideas of human liberty and representative government. The French Revolution of 1789 was far different from our own. The scholar Jonathan Israel has written many books on the historical period leading up to the revolution and the end of the Bourbon monarchy. He explains that the revolution was caused by all the philosophical ideas being published and publicly discussed in the decades before 1779. The ideas of the French philosophers like Diderot, Rousseau, and Voltaire contained "all the germs of the Revolution." Thus, to ignore intellectual debates, no matter how strange or nonsensical, is to miss the warning of what kind of ideological swing is on its way into politics.

Revolutions are fanned by ideas, but the merit of ideas is not all equal. The French Revolution brought so much destruction, so much sacrilege, and so much innocent bloodshed. The ideas of the American Revolution avoided these excesses because the enemy was not internal but a monarch across the sea, George III.

We mention this not as a history lesson but as a warning. Jonathan Israel goes on to explain that these ideas spread quickly through all the social classes in Paris because of the number of pamphlets being published daily. The ladies who forced Louis XVI and Marie Antoinette to leave the Versailles palace may have been ridiculed as sans-culottes,[1] but they had the words *liberté*, *égalité*, and *fraternité* (liberty, equality, and fraternity) on their lips and understood them.

---

[1]   The lower classes could not afford to wear the fashionable culottes worn by the upper classes.

2.

Just as there is the battle of ideas, there is the battle for law and order on the streets of our cities. Personal injuries and destroyed storefronts are being ignored for fear of the police or city hall being called *racist*. The media covers injuries attributed to white persons or the police, who are now considered defenders of "white privilege." Both Antifa and the violent wing of Black Lives Matter have attacked people, businesses, and the police across our nation with near impunity. Whatever happened to laws regarding disturbing the peace? Watching a screaming crowd converge on people dining *al fresco* or on shoppers trying to exit a grocery store is quite frightening, especially if you were one of those at dinner or shopping.

Black Lives Matter (BLM) received over $90 million[2] in donations in 2020 and was rewarded for its violence and for advocating positions such as the end to the "Western model" of the family. Celebrities became donors along with top corporations like Amazon, Apple, Coca-Cola, and Facebook.[3] How do you justify writing checks to an organization participating in looting and violence in major cities and the nation's capital? Is it any surprise that the bulk of those donations went to making Patrice Cullors, BLM's founder, and many other founders rich? Her personal finances and purchase of

[2] Lee Brown, "Black Lives Matter foundation received over $90M in donations last year," *The New York Post*, February 24, 2021, https://nypost.com/2021/02/24/black-lives-matter-received-over-90m-in-donations-last-year/.

[3] James Wellenmeyer, "Want to know where all those corporate donations for #BLM are going? Here's the list." *NBC News*, June 5, 2020, https://www.nbcnews.com/business/consumer/want-know-where-all-those-corporate-donations-blm-are-going-n1225371.

four homes for $3.2 million in the United States alone led to calls for investigation by her own BLM staff and ultimately to her resignation.[4] In addition, no one within BLM even knew how much money Cullors was raking in. This led Hawk Newsome of BLM Greater NYC to call for an investigation. It was the combination that prompted her to resign, which, naturally, she blamed on "racists" in the "right-wing media."

The problem of dealing with the violence and provocative behavior of Antifa neatly disappears when you deny the organization exists, like Joe Biden did in the 2020 presidential debates: "Antifa is an idea, not an organization," Biden said to Donald Trump in the debate.[5] Ideas don't break windows or turn over tables on sidewalk restaurants. People do.

Antifa is real; the modern American version of it intensified in Portland in 2007.[6] It operates in an Alinsky-like way, with individual groups organizing in major cities with no overall administration. What unites Antifa is its commitment to violence. At a February 2020 counter-demonstration in Portland, Antifa members desecrated a war memorial by spray-painting messages like "kill the cops" and "all Cops

---

[4]   Natalie O'Neill, "Black Lives Matter co-founder Patrisse Cullors resigns amid controversy," *The New York Post*, May 27, 2021, https://nypost.com/2021/05/27/black-lives-matter-co-founder -patrisse-cullors-resigns-amid-controversy/.

[5]   Julio Rosas, "Joe Biden Denies Antifa Organizations Exist," *Townhall*, September 29, 2020, https://townhall.com/tipsheet/juliorosas/2020/09/29/joe-biden-denies-antifa-is-an-organization-its-an -idea-n2577189.

[6]   Kyle Shideler, "The Real History of Antifa," *The American Mind*, June 6, 2020, https://americanmind.org/salvo/the-real-history-of -antifa/.

are Bastards."[7] This was after throwing concrete at the police and striking by-standers with umbrellas.

Elected officials in these cities fear being called "racist" more than they care about enforcing the law and protecting citizens and their property. How do you fight back when some police, attorneys general, and judges exert their political preferences rather than following the law?

3.

But the violence is not confined to these groups alone; it can break out anywhere and anytime they find a suitable target. President Trump's leading allies and their families faced an onslaught of death threats, damage to their property, and the presence of angry, screaming, and threatening protestors at their homes. Most of the physical harassment is generally unknown by the public because most of the Trump victims refuse to play the victim card.

This kind of violence, and worse, was part of both the Soviet and Nazi revolutions that took control of their respective nations. The breakdown in law and order allowed armed thugs to beat and kill anyone who stood in the way of their ideology. Property, of course, was confiscated by the new political bosses and the owners sent to "camps." Politicized government agencies, such as the IRS, FDA, DOJ, FBI, OSHA, and CDC, can do similar damage. If America cannot

---

[7]   Lauren Edmonds, "Antifa protestors throw concrete at police and vandalize a war memorial with 'Kill Cops' message during demonstration against a planned KKK rally in Portland," *Daily Mail*, February 9, 2020, https://www.dailymail.co.uk/news/article-798 4293/Antifa-protest-against-cancelled-KKK-rally-leads-three-arre sts-war-memorial-vandalized.html.

be a nation of laws, a nation following its Constitution, then there is no protection from those who have taken power.

We need to regard social media as a place to tread through carefully, fully aware of the kind of language and comment that can make you a target. Use social media strategically as a place you can argue and attempt to change minds, where you can engage in the battle of ideas.

During the summer of 2020, Black Lives Matter finally was able to grab America's attention in response to George Floyd's tragic death at the knee of a police officer in Minneapolis. America was at the breaking point as the Chinese coronavirus lockdown was having a negative impact on mental health generally.

I remember working from my home office (even though ACU was open every day) and watching the coverage on television. Months of inaccurate panicky Chinese coronavirus coverage was followed by strangely vague explanations of the violent riots that exploded all over America and in Washington, DC. I could not believe how many times good conservatives and Republicans on television would vaguely talk about "those" behind the riots for fear of social media and corporate media censors canceling future appearances due to critical statements about BLM, which these platforms equated to the NAACP. If the rioters were emblazoned with BLM shirts, masks, and water bottles, why was it wrong to simply make that clear?

I had to say something. I started to tweet my disgust at the idea of punishing all cops for the criminal actions of a small minority. The ACU staff then began to investigate the organizations behind BLM and their stated policy positions. The radicalism and Marxism oozed from the words, and all of it attacked the parts of society that offered hope for urban minority kids—namely, families, churches, and cessation of violent crime.

My tweets resulted in a well-orchestrated pressure campaign by Democrats to enlist a blogger whose intent was to ruin my commercial relationships. I remember reading an email from the blogger asking me for a comment. I knew as I fell asleep that night that my world would be turned upside down. If I had remained quiet, I would not have had to deal with being canceled. I had a disagreement inside my head. Had I damaged my five kids' financial security? Had I been egotistical to think my voice mattered and at such a grave cost? A few days later, I was alone in my office when I got a call from a client who I considered a friend.

"I'm going to have to let you go."

"What?"

"We are committed to racial equality and to Black Lives Matter, and you are not."

This person was a professed Christian and, in fact, was constantly reminding everyone about his devotion but was telling me that I had breached decency by criticizing BLM not on racial policies or the brutality of George Floyd's death, but for saying that BLM criticism of the nuclear family, the Christian Church, her saints, and the Old Testament foundation in support of the State of Isreal was offensive. Corporate America had been able to leverage its Christian executives to fire anyone who defended the church from vile public BLM attacks.

I realized that American corporate culture was in free fall. But the most cutting part of the exchange was a text this corporate persecutor sent afterwards asking if there were no hard feelings and if we could still be friends. Imagine your friend calls you out and accuses you of being a racist, lectures you on decency, fires you on vile false changes, condemns you for being a dedicated conservative, which was the reason he had viewed you has a valuable consultant in the first place, and at the end wants to be buddies and drink brewskies.

My response was quick. I did not wish to pretend that the vile sin of racism is a casual thing. If a friend believes me to be a racist, then he should not want to be my friend. The fact that this person wanted to still have our friendship unchanged proved that he knew his charge was false and I was a victim.

These examples demonstrate that oftentimes the corporations or established power structures do not actually care about combating racism. If they did, they would immediately suspend all funding of BLM until the organization rescinded obnoxious and harmful Marxist policy positions that are hostile to black moms and dads. There are countless families and black pastors who could have used the billions of dollars raised for Black Lives Matter, Inc. to help real people in crisis.

In these two examples, corporate go-betweens tried to deliver an unjust decision in a manner that attempted to gain my buy in. The lesson I learned is that despite the consequences, I have to follow my conscience. And if everyone who appeared on media could be forced into silence on BLM's Marxism and violence, the destruction of our cities and our communities will never end. It is critical in these moments that those who love America explain as clearly as possible that there will be no co-option with the dominant themes being pushed by social media oligarchs. They may wield immense power, including the powers to silence and destroy reputations, but our response to it can impact how they handle the next victim.

—Matt Schlapp

CHAPTER 12

The Heart of America

1.

Let's take a moment and ask ourselves what it is that we are losing in our nation. In other words, what's the bottom line? Personal liberty is at the heart of why America was born. It's easy to take this for granted, to forget its centrality, because we are centuries away from sophisticated societies ruled by kings and queens, landed-aristocracy, rigid class distinction, and church authorities with the power to arrest, imprison, and execute.

The first immigrants to America braved the ocean crossing in ships a hundred feet long and thirty feet wide in search of liberty. They had been persecuted for their version of the Christian faith or went in search of economic opportunity lacking in the old-world regimes. The meaning of American liberty can only be understood against the backdrop of the authoritarian power of nations like England, France, Spain, and Germany—especially that of George III, king of England in 1776. As Jefferson wrote about him in the Declaration of Independence, "The history of the present King

of Great Britain is a history of repeated injuries and usur-
pations, all having in direct object the establishment of an
absolute Tyranny over these States."[1]

The challenge of the American founding was to figure out
how a nation can be ruled without despotism. The United
States became the first experiment where founders wrote
down the explicit rights individuals had as their birthright.
They sought to build a nation that combined personal liberty with the necessities of a national government and its
laws. Jefferson put it this way: "to institute new Government,
laying its foundation on such principles and organizing its
powers in such form, as to them shall seem most likely to
affect their Safety and Happiness."

Notice how the "Safety and Happiness" of the citizenry is
the object of government, not the empowerment of an elite
class. Yet, by their very nature, all laws restrict personal freedom
in order to protect citizens from forms of injustice, including
theft, bodily harm, and loss of life. The Constitution of the
United States sought to protect personal liberty by creating a
governmental structure designed to keep power from accruing
to any single individual or any single institutional entity. The
Preamble to the US Constitution underscores the benefit of
democratic rule to each citizen. It designated the safety, liberty, and tranquility (happiness) of the people as the purpose
of government: "We the People of the United States, in Order
to form a more perfect Union, establish Justice, insure domestic Tranquility, provide for the common defense, promote the

---

[1]   "Declaration of Independence: A Transcription," National Ar-
        chives, July 24, 2020, https://www.archives.gov/founding-docs
        /declaration-transcript.

general Welfare, and secure the Blessings of Liberty to ourselves and our Posterity, do ordain and establish this Constitution for the United States of America."[2]

2.

Thus, the founders created a three-part government with both elected and appointed offices, with the key element being that all elected officers serve a limited term requiring them to run for reelection. "We the People" were to be given the chance to remove representatives and to replace them with those who respect the wishes of those who elect them. It's called accountability.

The first president, George Washington, refused to be treated like a king. After eight years of war and eight years away from his home in Mt. Vernon, Washington did not want the job but took it nonetheless for the sake of the nation. He did everything he could to rid the first inaugural ceremony of any pomp and ceremony befitting royalty. His decision not to wear his military uniform but a double-breasted brown suit was meant to dispel fears of a military-type rule.[3]

As Plato argued in *The Republic*, the best rulers are those who don't want to rule. The socialists, Democrats, and their allies thirst for political power, and they have less and less respect for personal liberty. Why? Because they want us to accept the

---

[2]   "The Constitution of the United States: A Transcription," National Archives, May 4, 2020, https://www.archives.gov/founding-docs/constitution-transcript.

[3]   Ron Chernow, "George Washington: The Reluctant President," *Smithsonian Magazine*, February 2011, https://www.smithsonianmag.com/history/george-washington-the-reluctant-president-49492/.

radical ideology they promote, to conduct our private lives according to their dictates, and to educate our children according to their distorted moral values and their secular worldview.

Their political thirst is witnessed everyday by the lies they propagate—remember the Steele Dossier[4]—and the double standard they apply to Republicans when it comes to accusations of personal scandal.[5] Justice Brett Kavanaugh and his family were put through a veritable hell of public scorn and humiliation by vicious accusations that no one (including the accuser) was able to confirm. By contrast, accusations toward President Biden and his family are shrugged off.

In other words, the Democrats have engaged in the sort of raw abuses of power that led our forefathers to the founding of America itself. It's not that they have forgotten the history of this nation; no, they reject it. They want to "cancel" the founders, the Declaration, and the Constitution.

We cannot allow the state to dictate the meaning of human existence, especially the centrality of the "domestic church,"[6] which is the family. America was founded as a nation where religious belief would not have to knuckle under to federal or state power. The First Amendment protection described as

---

[4] Jay Greenberg, "New York Times Admits Anti-Trump 'Steele Dossier' Was Fake," *Neon Nettle*, May 18, 2021, https://neonnettle.com/news/15276-new-york-times-admits-anti-trump-steele-dossier-was-fake.

[5] James M. Casey, "'Unmasking' Steele dossier source: Was confidentiality ever part of the deal?" *The Hill*, August 1, 2020, https://thehill.com/opinion/white-house/509645-unmasking-steele-dossier-source-was-confidentiality-ever-part-of-the-deal.

[6] Pope Paul VI, dogmatic constitution *Lumen Gentium* (November 21, 1964), chapter 11.

"religious liberty" was itself inspired by the Judeo-Christian principles held by the founders and framers.

What is it like to be called a racist continually? To see everything you hold dear and what you believe to be virtuous slandered as "bigotry"?

It is soul-crushing.

It makes you sad for the state of things, but eventually it just makes you mad. The problem with hatred generally is that it metastasizes. When a person who means well is slimed with the slur of racism, it angers both the one making the slanderous charge and the one who it is intended to publicly shame. There is no upside.

During our CPAC conference in 2021, there was a coordinated attack to label us not just as "white supremacists" but specifically as "Nazis."

It started when one of our invited speakers, who had been recommended by an ACU ally, was discovered to have posted terribly hurtful anti-Semitic comments. We should have scrutinized the speaker more diligently, but as soon as we were made aware of the comments, we rescinded the invitation.

That did not stop irresponsible voices in the mainstream media from saying the invite was a "dog whistle" to those intolerant supporters of racial purity and the architects of the disgraceful marches in Charlottesville that had occurred in August 2017.

It also spurred a round of mocking us for saying we were "Uncanceling America" while we were canceling a speaker. Of course, making prudent decisions on who can speak under severe time restrictions is called scheduling not silencing, but this is the game continually played by those in media providing cover for the cancel culturalists.

A stranger charge occurred as soon as our CPAC stage was completed when an aerial photograph was posted online claiming the stage had purposely been designed to vaguely mimic a diamondesque symbol what was used on Nazi uniforms.[7] Our executive vice president and I (with surnames Schneider and Schlapp) were completely bamboozled by this charge. How did such an image hit the internet so quickly almost before we saw the finished project? How could anyone know of any Nazi symbol resemblance? One of our employees studied anti-Semitism in college and he was unaware of the symbolism. Even the designer of the stage was himself Jewish.

We soon learned that hotel executives were being pressured to make a public statement distancing themsevles from the conference. Can you imagine running a major hotel during the pandemic practically begging for customers to come to your hotel and at the same time making your distaste for your largest customer well-known to the media? Astonishingly after all of the acrimony, this hotel chain bid on the very next CPAC. Major companies expect Americans who love America

---

[7]   Chelsea Steiner, "The CPAC Stage Design Is Literally a Nazi Symbol Because Republicans Are Not Even Trying To Hide It Anymore," MSN, February 27, 2021, https://www.msn.com/en-us /news/world/the-cpac-stage-design-is-literally-a-nazi-symbol-beca use-republicans-are-not-even-trying-to-hide-it-anymore/ar-BB1e 4RxZ.

to be constantly criticized and called out while at the same time they continue to expect us to support their commercial enterprises. The issue with this hotel chain is largely unique, and the chain has encouraged CPAC to have additional events at their various locations. Our message back to corporate America is our movement is seventy-five million strong and growing, if you want our business, you must treat us with the respect we deserve.

—Matt Schlapp

CHAPTER 13

This Has All Happened Before

1.

Our nation has already been captured once by moral zealots who "know what is better" for all Americans. Back then, however, the political pressure was applied from conservatives, primarily Protestants, who were members of over thirty temperance organizations such as the Anti-Saloon League, the Women's Christian Temperance Union, and the Ku Klux Klan. The support of the KKK demonstrated the anti-Catholic sentiment that motivated many of Prohibition's advocates at a time when Irish and German immigrants were coming to America. Approximately 4.5 million Irish immigrants came to America between 1820 and 1930.[1]

On January 16, 1920, the Volstead Act went into effect, prohibiting the illegal production and sale of liquor,

---

[1]   "Irish-Catholic Immigration to America," Library of Congress, accessed September 29, 2021, https://www.loc.gov/classroom-ma terials/immigration/irish/irish-catholic-immigration-to-america /%23:~:text=It%2520is%2520estimated%2520that%2520as,all.

including beer. Prohibition lasted an amazing thirteen years until the Twenty-First Amendment was passed.

Racism was also a real problem at the time, but the government regrettably did not intervene.[2]

Looking back, however, it's clear that alcoholism was wreaking havoc on families throughout the country. Part of this problem was due to the drinking habits brought by the Irish, German, and other European immigrants. Alcoholism was a real problem, though other factors must have been involved because present alcohol consumption per person is higher than it was in 1920: 2 gallons per teen and adult vs. 2.3 gallons.[3]

What's pertinent to note is the total absence of the principle of subsidiarity—meaning that social problems should first be addressed at the local level before being handed over to any level of government, whether city, county, state, or federal. The use of "mediating institutions" such as churches, hospitals, schools, and groups devoted solely to treating alcoholism were not relied upon to deal with the problem.

2.

The history of the Roaring Twenties, with the rise of criminal organizations based upon bootlegging, was the direct result of the federal take-over. Such a foolish social experience also diminished respect for law, the police, and the

---

[2]   "Prohibition," History, October 29, 2009, https://www.history .com/topics/roaring-twenties/prohibition.

[3]   Mike Stobbe, "US drinking more now than before Prohibition," *AP News*, January 14, 2020, https://apnews.com/article/public-he alth-health-statistics-health-us-news-ap-top-news-f1f81ade07484 10aaeb6eeab7a772bf7.

judicial system. Prohibition was the most widely flouted law in the history of America, with the possible exception of speed limits.

Many who defied Prohibition became wealthy and powerful; few suffered from law enforcement. But today's defiance by the "woken" oligarchy, all the experts, wise men, and shamans, who command talk shows, the nightly news, and the opinion sections of major newspapers is altogether different; they don't like being challenged. They are doing their best to make any disobedience to their established dogma come at a cost. In fighting back, the first thing to realize is there may be a cost to pay. No one can overcome fear if they constantly avoid risk and suffering. That's how fear holds us prisoner.

We have already witnessed private citizens—restaurant owners, bakers, pastors, priests, actors, musicians, politicians—who have paid a price. We watched for four years as our president and his entire family was treated to daily floggings in the media, not only in the United States, but internationally. He may no longer be president, but the same media and rabid anti-Trumpers are trying to destroy his hotel business, his golf courses, and shut down his future opportunities. The media have tried to make the name Trump equivalent to Hitler. And its effort will not stop.

Those of us who support Trump will be treated like those who admired what Hitler did to Germany and the Jews. On the top of that, we will be called racists, ignoramuses, domestic terrorists, insurrectionists, and any other toxic label they can slap on us.

The desecrators, we should recognize, are already suffering from the law of unintended consequences. Ironically, silencing Trump's Twitter account may have put him back on the road to rehabilitation and certainly has made him a sympathetic figure to red America, and maybe to any honest old-school ACLU types, if any still remain alive or are brave enough to buck this left-wing fascism.

The effort to silence a prominent conservative voice is an example of the cancel culture executed with true French revolutionary zeal. In the hands of the desecrators, this cancellation has no boundaries and can descend on anyone who fights back at any time.

We should take as our inspiration and model the patriots at the Second Continental Congress (convened in 1775). In response to the British occupation of Boston and another wave of imposed taxation (specifically on tea), associations began to be organized in all the colonies. These associations became the locus of preparation for resistance to state power and abuse.

> The years I attended high school, 1964–1967, were the most turbulent years of the Civil Rights Movement. Martin Luther King Jr. was assassinated in 1968 during my freshman year at the University of Texas. I remember watching the news report on a TV screen in the cafeteria feeling bewildered at the hate that ended in his death.
> —Deal W. Hudson

CHAPTER 14

Prohibition Returns

1.

What the Democrats and the oligarchy of intellectuals, media, industry leaders, and globalists envision is far worse than Prohibition. They want to create a new society by reeducating Americans, especially our children, and in doing so cancel what lies at the heart of America—its commitment to the protection of liberty: freedom of speech, freedom of thought and expression, freedom of religion, and the freedom of parents to educate their children.

Christianity, which has been the dominant religion of America since its beginning, is now being legally labeled as a source of hatred.[1] As such, Christians who articulate their views on sexual morality are subject to prosecution for hate crimes. What is the crime? You've made someone feel threatened, uncomfortable, rejected. You've hurt their feelings and sense of self-worth. It's laughable, right? But criminalizing

---

[1]   Deal W. Hudson, "The Coming Tsunami of 'Hate Speech' Legislation," *Crisis Magazine*, December 18, 2020, https://www.crisismagazine.com/2020/the-coming-tsunami-of-hate-speech-legislation.

the speech that makes others feel threatened is already an established reality.

The laughable, the ridiculous, and the pathetic have all been made a matter of public policy by socialists, Democrats, and their oligarch class. We are on the way to the Soviet form of life in which every word or facial expression has to be managed in order to avoid the accusation of committing a crime against "the Party."

Millions of Americans have been using social media for years in a variety of silly or obnoxious ways, all the while not knowing one day they will be held to account. Every day we read about people whose lives have been destroyed by something they said or did years ago that has been put on the internet.

2.

Take Mimi Groves, who foolishly used the N-word on a form of social media, Snapchat, that was supposed to disappear shortly after posting.[2] She had sent it to a bi-racial friend who saved it and deliberately posted it three years later after Mimi was accepted to the University of Tennessee and made the cheerleading squad. Very quickly, she was cut from the cheerleaders and the university recommended that she withdraw, which she did.

Her so-called friend, Jimmy Galligan, is proud of what he did: "I wanted to get her where she would understand the severity of that word." Imagine a world where all we say and do as tenth graders follows us around for the rest of our

---

[2]   Elizabeth Elizalde, "White teen pushed out of college after video of her saying N-word at 15 resurfaces," *The New York Post*, December 29, 2020, https://nypost.com/2020/12/29/white-teen-kicked-out-of-college-after-n-word-video-resurfaces/.

lives! For that matter, how many tenth graders understand the power of the social media they are using each day?

Who, whether out of immaturity, anger, drunkenness, or plain stupidity, has not said things that should have never been said? Nobody, not even those who have created a social climate where anyone can use the internet to destroy the life and reputation of anyone, whether out of spite, envy, or a misguided sense of moral duty.

What the Soviet Union and the French Reign of Terror had in common was the deputizing of the citizenry to report on friends and neighbors for speech and thought crimes. But now these reports don't have to go through a court of any kind—all that has to be done is to post a video or audio deemed "offensive," and the knives of elite media will immediately come out, mercilessly.

Those who opposed the Prohibition of the 1920s found a way to consume liquor in spite of the law. What is it that we must do to oppose the dictatorial shamers and the arrogant academics who desecrate history? The desecrators are trying to prohibit truth-telling the way the puritans of the '20s made liquor consumption illegal.

My favorite part is when an apostle of the dark arts of cancel culture calls you a bigot and then in turn is insulted and offended when you yell back at them in defense of your honor. It's as if they expect that the rules of the game are well understood, and the conservative victim will simply take it like a man or a household pet.

Recall my example in a previous chapter about the charges of racism that get bandied around during

CPAC? The moralizing on race becomes so unattached from fighting real bigotry that when they throw around the words *Nazi* or *Fascism*, they no longer use the term anti-Semitism. Why? Because the Left has long ago abandoned fighting anti-Semitism as Israel is now propagandized as the oppressor of and squatters on the Palestinians and their lands.

The persecutor of woke punishment expects the persecuted to simply take the public humiliation and slink away into the shadows to do the time in the penalty box before making public pronouncements of how insensitive the person allegedly had been. This is the game Hollywood and Wall Street play. A noted person with an important job does something terrible, and now humiliated, the noted person goes to some type of sensitivity training, gets a tan, and reemerges a few months later perfectly woke and repentant.

And make no mistake, they are coming for each and every one of us. In fact, I remind the employees of these corporate entities that fired me during the long, nasty summer that if holding very mainstream Republican views, like respect for the words of Martin Luther King Jr. or the need for voter ID, could be considered dangerous, then each of them would be brought up on charges within their own companies one day and would be a future victim.

I also warned that their corporate PACS would soon be unable to support the GOP, which is the center-right party still willing to work with corporations on tax cuts, regulation roll back, strict constructionist judges, and the rule of law generally. Sadly, by the beginning of 2021, most US public companies had indeed frozen contributions to over one hundred national Republicans after they raised very legitimate questions about the legal process of mail-in ballots and the bizarre 2020 election.

Perhaps there is no way to stop the thirst for political blood from anyone who loves America, her founding, her heroes, her history, and her traditional institutions. But it seems clear that we must, when we can, shame them back for their complicity in the destruction of civil society.

—Matt Schlapp

CHAPTER 15

Turning the Tide

1.

A book like this only succeeds when it enlightens, persuades, and impacts behavior. We have explained how the United States Constitution itself is being ignored, how the Declaration's rights of "life, liberty, and the pursuit of happiness" are no longer regarded as "unalienable," and how we can work individually and together to turn the tide of a growing despotism.

Do we agree with Patrick Henry who said, "Give me liberty or give me death"? Of course! But remember, Henry was challenging the authority of the British crown already determined to round up, imprison, and execute traitors. America has not reached such an impasse, though there is considerable violence on our nation's streets, and we pray the temptation of another revolution or civil war will never possess the public imagination. However, we have witnessed the nascent movements towards secession in several states, which does not bode well for a peaceful future.

Political engagement is the moral duty of all Americans. We sympathize with those who have chosen to disengage from what they consider a toxic culture to protect their sanity and their children. But their duty as American citizens to political participation does not come to an end; we have a nation to defend and to protect. The well-being of future generations demands that we do all we can do.

2.

It's not a matter of insipid nostalgia to look back at the images of men and women slain in combat since the time of one of the first casualties of the American Revolution on March 5, 1770. His name was Crispus Attucks, a black man from Boston who was a sailor and rope maker.[1] Over a million Americans have died defending our nation from its enemies both internal and foreign.[2] If you have seen the opening minutes of the film *Saving Private Ryan* (1998), you saw men, some very young, being shot down before they could exit the boats which brought them to Normandy Beach. You saw them swim and struggle towards the machine guns in concrete bunkers firing down upon them as their buddies were being torn to pieces all around them.

They fought against a fanatical power that had stripped the nation of Germany of its most basic liberties and subjected most of Europe to dictatorial and genocidal rule. These soldiers

---

[1]   "Crispus Attucks," Biography, March 26, 2021, https://www.bio graphy.com/military-figure/crispus-attucks.

[2]   Laura Santhanam, "How many Americans have died in U.S. wars?" *PBS News Hour*, May 27, 2019, https://www.pbs.org/news hour/nation/many-americans-died-u-s-wars.

fought to defend a set of ideas that has created a nation and a way of life unique in the history of the world. What they sacrificed for future generations cannot be calculated.

In the third year of a bloody civil war, President Abraham Lincoln expressed the hope that future generations would enjoy a nation still "conceived in liberty, and dedicated to the proposition that all men are created equal."[3] If Lincoln could express this vision at such a tragic moment, all are remiss who cannot do the same right now.

It is often said that politics lies downstream from culture. But that's simplistic. Politics can influence societal norms and attitudes through its legislation, budgetary priorities, court cases, and public debate. Defeating the desecrators requires political involvement, or we will be dealing with legislation like the Equality Act, packing the Supreme Court, federalizing election law, and eliminating state regulations on abortions for decades to come.

> After the election, when President Trump, through Ambassador Ric Grenell, had asked me to travel to Nevada to help manage election challenges, I found myself in Carson City at a tiny hotel, which of course had a little casino in the lobby (we were in Nevada, after all). Nothing could be more depressing than a night on the town in Vegas during the socialist shutdown in November and December. But Carson City was worse.
>
> I ordered a cup of coffee early one morning. I was sipping my liquid breakfast when a crusty old timer

---

[3] "The Gettysburg Address," HistoryNet, accessed September 29, 2021, https://www.historynet.com/gettysburg-address-text.

recognized me from Hannity appearances. He encouraged me to get honest election results, and we parted with that special bond that exists between those who know the trouble America is in. I looked around as about a dozen gamblers, almost all well past their prime, tried to smoke, drink, and gamble while wearing a mandated mask.

A security guard walked up and told me I had to reapply my mask after each sip of coffee. I told him that touching a mask ran contrary to all the guidelines which explicitly warn people to not have their hands touch their face or mask. We went round and round. I was not going to take off and reapply my mask. Ever. Enough was enough.

Finally, he said all this was "crap," but he needed to police the geriatric gamblers or he would lose his job. The left-wing governor had undercover agents enforcing his insanely harsh crackdown complete with multiple thousand-dollar fines and churches closed but the casinos opened. Now he had me. I knew what it meant to be worried about employment. I put my hand on his shoulder and told him I would leave and drink my coffee in my room, with a broken television and a leaky window.

I then spoke in a loud voice that echoed around the mostly empty casino. I said the masks were not keeping us healthy; they were keeping us down. I told them their governor was oppressing them and that the mask mandate of today could be the beginning of us losing our country. I urged them to stand up. I was fired up.

As I walked away, a few old codgers nodded in agreement; others looked away. Everyone knew the whole scene was a pathetic example of individual Americans trying to find a little pleasure in a dark time.

I had endured a brutal 2020. I lost many long-time commercial relationships. I lost more friends. I had been accused of racism so harshly that I wondered if I had anything left to offer. I was caught up in an insanely disorganized attempt to expose illegal ballots.

But in all the pain, there was a calling, to get up to listen and find a way. I kept wondering if George Washington and Abraham Lincoln and Christopher Columbus and Booker T. Washington were watching America. What side were the statues on? The men and women who lived heroic lives must have an opinion on the direction of America. Were they in glory in heaven rooting the good guys on who saw the evils of socialism? Who can know for sure, but at that moment, I had little left to lose. There were only two things I clung to: my family and an earnest attempt to find a path in a jungle of confusion, personal pain, and societal chaos, with God's grace.

—Matt Schlapp

CHAPTER 16

Using Symbols Is a Must!

1.

How many people do you know who told you they were afraid to put Trump/Pence signs in their yards during the last presidential campaign? There were more than a few reports of property destruction and violence against those who did.[1] In Colorado, a grown woman made a U-turn in her moped in order to punch repeatedly a twelve-year-old for holding a Trump sign.[2] Another woman arriving at a rented home in Maine was shocked by the presence of Trump signs, "I immediately was terrified and scared for my life and family safety."[3]

---

[1]   Elizabeth Rosner, "Dispute over Trump yard sign in Kansas leaves 3 injured," *Fox News*, November 2, 2020, https://www.foxnews .com/us/shot-dispute-trump-yard-sign-kansas.

[2]   Ewan Pamer, "Woman Repeatedly Punches 12-year-old Boy for Carrying Trump 2020 Sign, Police Say," *Newsweek*, September 3, 2020, https://www.newsweek.com/colorado-boy-assaulted-trump -sign-1529382.

[3]   Greg Holt, "Woman Fears for Her Life After Seeing Trump Yard Signs," *News With Views*, September 30, 2020, https://newswith views.com/woman-fears-for-her-life-after-seeing-trump-yard-si gns/.

Sporting fans have been dealing with athletes choosing to kneel during the playing of the national anthem. Their expressed purpose in kneeling is protesting the treatment of African Americans in America.[4] Quarterback Colin Kaepernick is credited with starting it all when he sat on the bench while the national anthem was being played one day in August 2016.

"Taking the knee" soon spread to other sports, especially basketball, where celebrity athletes such as LeBron James considered it mandatory that his fellow NBA players kneel before every game.[5] Internal debates arose at the owner and administrative level of the NFL and NBA, both of which eventually caved under pressure from the big-name players and the media to allow kneeling. As a result, their TV ratings plummeted because fans were angered by the politicization of viewing—many of these fans for years have planned their time around watching basketball and football.[6]

National symbols, like those of religion, can have an explosive effect when they are disrespected. What was sad to see, however, were the numerous people who were cowered by the Black Lives Matter protests. BLM does not stop at peaceful protests like those who "take the knee." BLM's

---

4   Joanne Kavanagh, "Raising Awareness Taking the knee history: What is the meaning and origin of the gesture?" *The Sun*, June 20, 2020, https://www.thesun.co.uk/news/11771451/take-a-knee-meaning-history-blm/.

5   "NBA: LeBron James leads Black Lives Matter protests as season starts," BBC, July 31, 2020, https://www.bbc.com/sport/basketball/53580644.

6   Vincent Frank, "NBA Playoffs: TV ratings down a stunning amount from last season," *Sportsnaut*, October 1, 2020, https://sportsnaut.com/nba-playoffs-tv-ratings/.

prominence exploded after the shooting of George Floyd on May 26, 2020. The group's very effective upraised fist symbol was inspired by the US Olympian John Carlos, who in the 1968 games raised a black-gloved fist on the podium after receiving his bronze medal in the 200-meter sprint.[7]

The fist along with the letters *BLM* were suddenly being spray-painted on roads and buildings throughout the United States. In Washington, DC, 16th Street in front of the White House was turned into "Black Lives Matter Plaza," with the name painted on the street in large yellow letters. DC Mayor Muriel Browser decided to create this kitschy symbolic tribute on her own without much or any consultation. You must admit that these activists understand the power of symbols and don't hesitate to use them.[8]

While BLM and Antifa protests were destroying the downtown sections of cities like Seattle, Portland, Minneapolis, and Louisville, many Trump supporters were fretting over whether to put signs in their front yard. These supporters demonstrated exuberantly when at Trump rallies, where there was safety in numbers. On the other hand, many hesitated to demonstrate their support at home where hostile neighbors might tear down their sign or worse.

---

[7]   Debbie White, "Black Lives Matter fist symbol – what's the meaning behind the Black Power salute?" *The Sun*, June 3, 2020, https://www.thesun.co.uk/news/11761639/black-lives-matter-fist -symbol-meaning-black-power-salute/.

[8]   "Black Lives Matter Plaza: What Is The BLM Plaza And Where Is It Located?" Capitol FM, June 12, 2020, https://www.capitalfm.com /news/black-lives-matter-plaza-where/.

2.

What would happen, for instance, if the seventy-four million citizens who voted for Trump started displaying an American flag 365 days of the year? There would be incidents, yes, but in the long haul, it would demonstrate visually that the country does not belong to the cancel culture crowd. Such a gesture would have the symbolic power of lessening the fear of standing alone in a hostile neighborhood.

Obviously, the American flag stands for much more than Trump support or even support of conservative values. The flag represents all Americans, whether they kneel or not, reminding them of our nation's history and, particularly, the drama of its coming-into-being. Anyone who reads a history of America, from the Boston Tea Party in 1773 to the framing of the Constitution in 1789 and the War of 1812, will become acutely aware of how the nation barely avoided destruction.

We have already mentioned the decisive importance of Washington's victories at Trenton and Princeton, but another man, hardly known at all, played a similar role in the War of 1812. After burning most of Washington, DC, including the White House and the Capitol on August 24, 1814, British troops led by Major General Robert Ross and Admiral Alexander Cochrane sailed their frigates with four thousand soldiers north to Baltimore Bay with the intention of taking Philadelphia.

Had it not been for Samuel Smith (1752–1839), it's very likely the British would have succeeded and taken back their lost colony.[9] Smith was a former Maryland congressman and officer in the Revolutionary War. He anticipated the arrival of the British, and as major general of the Maryland militia, he mobilized thousands of men and built additional fortifications. When Ross tried to disembark four thousand men, they were delayed long enough by Baltimore militia for them to retreat to a fortified position where Smith had stationed the remainder of his militiamen.

The Battle of Baltimore was won because this one man, seeing the lack of preparation by the adversary, took charge, commanding the militia and artillery that decisively sent the British ships back where they came from.

The simultaneous naval assault by Admiral Cochrane of Fort McHenry, of course, was the occasion of Francis Scott Key's famous poem set to the tune of an old drinking song—"To Anacreon in Heaven"—which became the national anthem. Key was inspired by the raising of the battered American flag, forty-two by thirty feet, by the soldiers of the fort who had endured twenty-five hours of constant shelling.

We wonder what LeBron James and the rest of the kneelers would have to say if they came face-to-face with the garrison of Fort McHenry, its commander, Major George Armistead, and a force of around one thousand men.

If cancel culture is to be defeated, it will be necessary for Americans to reappropriate the national symbols that are being mocked and turned into symbols of racial hatred.

---

9   "Samuel Smith of Baltimore," War of 1812 Archaeology, (blog) July 15, 2013, https://warof1812archaeology.blogspot.com/2013/07 /samuel-smith-of-baltimore.html.

Think of seventy-four million American flags being displayed across our nation every day of the year, not just Flag Day. It would make a difference.

When asked in 1999 to lead Governor Bush's Catholic outreach, I assumed the chief obstacle to overcome was the deeply embedded loyalty to a distorted version of the "seamless garment" found in many of the Catholic institutions of our nation. Under this brand, the Catholic concern for the most poor and vulnerable among us was being used, if not to dismiss outright, at least hide out of sight the issue of abortion. Why this happened to the venerable Catholic understanding of social justice has been chronicled numerous times, but the bottom line is this: when the Democratic Party made the ideological issues of secular feminism a litmus test for party loyalty, millions of Catholics, including thousands of clergy, had to make a choice.

As a result of this choice, the Catholic voter was destabilized. No longer reliable Democrats, some Catholics became registered Republicans, and many became de facto independents or swing voters. Although at present there are still more self-identified Democrats among Catholic voters, the history of the presidential elections since the late '60s exhibits a level of volatility capable of swinging the election back and forth between the two major political parties.

By focusing on the swing Catholic voters who attended Mass regularly, Bush was very successful in 2000 and 2004 in regaining the Catholic support lost to the Democrats during the Clinton years. Senator John McCain made little effort in this regard, while Barack Obama's religious outreach team did an outstanding job of selling a pro-abortion candidate to Catholics as a president who would "lower" the abortion rate.

I initiated an effort called Catholic Advocate in 2006 with the hope of continuing independently the work of identifying, educating, and organizing Catholic voters. After six years, I handed it off to the next generation of leadership. Though I hope in the future to begin addressing once again a wider range of religious and cultural issues, there is one lesson I learned that I feel compelled to share: the problem of what I will call "the clerical frown."

There is a widespread inclination among US Catholics to ask their priest or their bishop for permission to become politically active, beyond the simple obligation of voting on Election Day. Thus, the problem I describe could also be called an improper form of lay deference, though I'm equally struck by how often those lay Catholics who sought guidance were met not by an explicit veto but by a gesture of disapproval—that is, the clerical frown.

Catholics have highly developed antennae, I have learned, for when Father is displeased, and many of them allow that displeasure to shape their attitudes and action in the political sphere. Obviously, when it comes to the teachings of the Church, the laity is constantly being taught and formed by our clergy and bishops. But does the teaching of the Church extend to decisions by the laity about whether to be a Republican or a Democrat, or to become active in an independent group like Catholic Advocate, the Susan B. Anthony List, or National Right to Life?

I am writing this to and for grown-ups. We all know that much human communication, including that between priests and laity, is exercised without the explicit language of yes and no. And since priests are just as human as the rest of us, they must be allowed gut reactions when asked for their opinions on any topic, whether it be politics, baseball, or the latest movie sequel. But our clergy surely know the power they wield with their body language and facial expressions, much less their praise and condemnations.

The solution is twofold: Lay Catholics simply need to affirm their obligation to engage fully in the political process without asking for permission from their pastor or their bishop. The Church itself teaches that prior permission is not required but that participation should be guided by the teaching of the Holy Father and the bishops. The clerical frown, as I call it, should be retired in regard to political matters. Catholic political participation is too important a matter to be disturbed by the political party preferences of our clergy. The Church does not care if a Catholic is a Democrat or a Republican; she cares about the work that is being done under that, or another, banner.

—Deal W. Hudson

CHAPTER 17

Trump Never Wavered

1.

As the 2016 election became the Trump presidency, there was a steady drumbeat from the media that there was something deranged about Donald Trump and his supporters. The "Make America Great Again" slogan was characterized as "white nationalism," as anti-immigrant, and as America only. Donald Trump, in turn, never stepped away from the controversy his words and actions created; instead, he embraced it. Trump did not backpedal; he did not apologize; he doubled down on the policies he wanted to change. It is not unusual for politicians to be reluctant to apologize. George W. Bush avoided spending time on mistakes, as it was perceived that presidential wallowing was akin to Jimmy Carter-like malaise.

Trump and his family have borne a tremendous cost for raising their heads and for taking on Washington. But the ultimate cost to individual supporters can be career ending. Most are not wealthy or powerful. They have a lot to lose for their support of Trump. There was never a time when you could just be a Trump supporter like some had been a Kemp or Dole supporter twenty years earlier. Supporting Trump, even saying positive things about him or his presidency, are still seen as fighting words.

For my wife and me, the 2016 election began an unrelenting cycle of losing friendships. I was surprised that for many in politics, friendships are secondary to career enhancements. This shocked me because politics is all about people: relating to them and partnering with them. The friends I made on the Todd Tiahrt congressional campaigns and the Bush/Cheney campaigns were among those I valued most. When you work extremely long hours, eat together, work out together, laugh together, and win together, there is a special bond that forms.

But supporting Donald Trump was altogether different. Dozens of friends never even confronted me personally over their opposition. Many broke up our friendship on Twitter! I suppose I am a sucker because twenty-four hours before the severing of the relationship, I would have taken their call and done anything for them.

After all this turmoil, my mom said it the best: "Son, they were never really your friends to begin with." True.

2.

For several years before the 2016 cycle, Mercy had been consulting for Barbara Bush and her wonderful foundation which encouraged higher literacy rates, a cause the former first lady championed throughout her public life. Mercy cherished those interactions and her time supporting a worthy cause. Jeb Bush was quite involved in the foundation, and when he announced for the presidency in 2016, he had removed himself from the nonprofit.

I was the chairman of the American Conservative Union, and putting on our massive annual conference, CPAC, required neutrality amongst the candidates as they each had to trust that the organization would not use CPAC in an unfair way. Mercy's role with the Barbara Bush Foundation made overt partisan activity more difficult. Therefore, neutrality seemed the prudent course.

However, for each of us, there were pressures to say and do things that would inch us closer to being involved and favoring a candidate. This pressure was most intense from the Bush world, including the Bush campaign staff. This tension resulted in a no-win situation for Mercy. If she said something complimentary of Jeb, or critical, then one side or the other was aggrieved. The Barbara Bush Foundation ended up canceling her contract. It did so, ironically enough, for her seeming too close to the Bush campaign.

Both Mercy and I continued to stay neutral but say positive things about Donald Trump, coupled with honest reactions to some of his statements. It was clear that Trump understood the moment we were living. Trump was quickly figuring out how to be a candidate, and we were trying to figure out how to give honest commentary and keep the respect and friendship of our former colleagues. As political commentators in the media, we wanted to play it straight.

Well, it was impossible. Many who viewed themselves as close to the Bush family were upset with us for not endorsing Governor Jeb Bush, who after a promising start and impressive fundraising, seemed to not understand that he needed to run as an outsider. Instead, he seemed to readily defend DC Republican leaders and their status quo.

As his campaign faltered, Governor Bush and his team decided on an ill-advised "Jeb Can Fix It!" slogan. He chose to emphasize a hearkening back to past bipartisanship and a friendlier time. We loved the idea of going back to a more mannerly DC existence, but I remember telling Mercy: "I don't want to 'fix' it, I want to make it all stop by taking it apart! Timber!"

Trump of course instinctively understood that Republicans wanted to break up DC's power, not fine-tune the DC bureaucracy.

3.

The 2016 Republican field was large and impressive.

The two easiest to deal with were Trump and Cruz. Trump usually called me personally or sent now-famous scans of notes when he wanted to discuss CPAC or politics. Cruz and his team responded immediately that they would be at CPAC events and also wanted a sit down to walk through every conceivable way he could take full advantage of the conference. They got it.

Carly Fiorina was serving as our American Conservative Union Foundation chair and had become quite a close friend. I encouraged her to consider running for president sometime during CPAC 2015. She had impressed me as one of the smartest people I had ever met; she was fun and engaging and looking for a great cause after having served as a CEO and losing a US Senate race in California. She also appeared to be a genuine conservative, despite many indicators that would lead some to the opposite conclusion.

So the batch of 2016 candidates was large, impressive, and filled with complexity for my wife and me. Rick Santorum, Carly, and Ted Cruz (who I had worked with in Austin when campaigning for George W. Bush) were long-term friends. Donald Trump was a very charismatic and intriguing outsider. Jeb Bush was the leading contender and an extension of our careers in the Bush White House. Scott Walker's campaign was being managed by a close friend. Marco Rubio was the son of Cuban immigrants from Miami, whom we had publicly supported over Charlie Crist at a time when his success seemed extremely unlikely.

To this day, I am impressed with the grace extended us by Senators Cruz and Santorum. Each could have really pressed the friendship to get more help for their race, but neither ever took advantage of such sentiment. It was clear we were in a tough spot, and perhaps they knew it.

Looking back on the 2016 field and recalling my own analysis of what it would take to secure the nomination, my overriding sense was that whoever captured the outsider lane and was able to convince enough in the establishment that they had a real chance of winning would become the nominee. Therefore, those candidates who had never won political office previously but had access to wealthy donors and other elites could make a real run for it especially after eight years of a rookie president with scant political experience and an overriding radical philosophy that severely divided the country.

That's why Dr. Ben Carson, Carly Fiorina, and Donald Trump all became top tier candidates, and the politicians who were most associated with fighting the ruling power in Washington DC and New York City all lead at one point or another, including Senator Ted Cruz and Governor Scott Walker. However, it was clear the candidate who was the least orthodox, the least establishment, the most offensive to the political ruling class, and the most impenetrable by their attacks was Donald Trump. When Mercy and I sat in the front of the arena in Cleveland, Ohio, during the first debate, Trump stood out. He was unafraid to answer his critics. He embraced his political incorrectness, and we all remember his brutal honesty in being the only person to say that he may not support the eventual nominee. All the others pledged that they would support the nominee, and many never supported Donald Trump.

4.

Heading into CPAC 2016, a group of GOP consultants began an aggressive Twitter campaign to pressure ACU into disinviting Trump due to his lack of a conservative record. Most of the activities came from the Rubio camp, and many were friends from the Bush days. The effort was unrelenting and personal. The more I interacted with the establishment candidates, the more I realized that I was turned off by their approach. They wanted a return to how things were done in the old days. They chafed about any conversations of illegal immigration besides "pathways to citizenship." They believed China was our ally and America would be made strong by shedding "dirty" manufacturing jobs. They mouthed cultural traditions but would never actually advise their candidates to do anything about them.

Being attacked on social media by people you thought respected you was tough. At that time, I felt obliged to respond to all the nastiness, each and every one. I remember one early morning I had stayed up to digitally defend myself. My wife walked up to me, grabbed my phone, and said "enough."

In an ironic twist, Donald Trump did end up skipping CPAC 2016, perhaps thinking that the Cruz factions would dominate the proceedings. Trump's campaign made some demands we could not accommodate and decided to skip the event at the last minute. Painfully, they instead flew to my hometown to have an event before the Kansas caucus. Trump would lose that caucus and the CPAC straw poll, ironically run by ACU board member Kellyanne Conway, but in many ways, the conservative movement was Trump's for the taking as he eventually earned all the delegates he needed. And for me personally, Trump was also always polite and never made it personal during these awkward moments. In fact, that night, he held a press conference and had nothing but nice things to say about me personally and the support of the conference. I think Trump realized more than he gets credit for that he needed the help of others to secure his ultimate goal of winning the presidency. Yes, he picks fights along the way, but they are more strategic than the media will ever give him credit for.

The long road to the GOP convention in Cleveland had resulted in widespread support for Donald Trump. He won in almost every primary and caucus. He lost in Iowa but recovered in New Hampshire and never looked back. His team was tight and a bit unconventional, but he had fast-moving advantages, a triple threat: a jet, a phone, and a voice.

Trump even won in the states which should have been dominated by favorite sons. Trump won in Florida, despite it being the base of power for Bush and Rubio, and he made Governor John Kasich sweat in Ohio. In fact, there was a time when a presidential candidate from a big state would dominate the delegate court; Trump ended all of that.

What began to emerge was a silent Trump supporter. Trump almost always outperformed his polls because most of the media coverage centered on his rhetoric aimed at his base, which was almost always equated to "racism," and a much-maligned populism, which was equated to demagoguery. This silent support could be seen rather constantly throughout the primary, the general election, and into the beginning of the Trump administration.

During a trip to Philadelphia, I attended an event populated by politicos and consultants. Usually at such events, I can easily float amongst groups and join conversations. I love interacting with people and making everyone feel comfortable. On this occasion, something happened I have only seen in movies. A group of consultants were in an animated conversation, and when I joined the circle, the conversation ended and there were lots of downcast looks at tasseled loafers. It was clear that whatever they were discussing, they did not want me to hear. It was an eye opener. Even seasoned Republican political hands were going to fight Trump to the end.

5.

Soon after the election, I went to a nursery to get a Christmas tree for our home. I am infamous in my family for playing up Christmas big, and I was trying to find the perfect tree. I had been to this nursery for over ten years but had always kept a low profile along with a large bill. While in line, an attractive woman who I knew owned or managed the place asked me to step out of line to talk with her. All I could think of was a Northern Virginia woke businesswoman wanting to ask me to leave her store because of my public support for Trump. I cringed, internally anticipating the verbal blows. You never get used to it.

She looked to her left and right and then looked me in the eyes and told me in hushed tones she loved Trump and was proud to have me in her store. She said that she had taken a long journey to become a conservative and now she tried to explain why government solutions usually just don't work to her employees. She then called over two black men to join our little huddle. Each was an immigrant, and each also had great affection for Donald Trump. We hung close together, laughing and enjoying our new bond. We were whispering our favorite Trump stories when our whispering became obvious. I wondered if they meant to be so discreet.

I asked the others why we were whispering. After all, we had a right to ardently vocalize support for our candidate. The owner explained that most of her clientele would not be amused, which of course was true in a blue-ing Virginia. I immediately thought of what it would be like to own a store near a big city. My desire to be financially successful would probably also keep me mostly hushed.

I remember loading up the tree, wreaths, and other Christmas gear and thinking how shocking the exchange was. I had been complimented and criticized many times in public. Most CNN and MSNBC viewers would complement me not on my opinions but on my manners. Fox viewers were almost always so encouraging. Sometimes I heard people murmuring about me, but no one every physically assaulted me or felt they could not speak freely. But this was the first time someone recognized me, sought me out, and then had a whole conversation in hushed tones.

What did I learn from this beautiful interaction? That whispering occurred when Trump supporters simply had to express themselves when normally they would simply be quiet. The whisper was their only outlet, and if it had been any other candidate, they would be shouting their support. The branding of Trump as outside the bounds of acceptable behavior had not destroyed his support but simply driven that support to be more careful. I realized when it came to Donald Trump, polling would always be a challenge.

6.

Mercy and I would encounter more Trump whisperers in the coming months. Oftentimes when I traveled to New York City and would stay in a hotel, a doorman or steward would come up, grab my bag, and whisper how much they loved Trump and liked me for defending him. The first few times, I thought it was great; after a dozen or so similar experiences, I realized immigrants and people of color had a special affection for Donald Trump and for those who stood by him. It was clear that the Republican approach of the past of pandering to minorities was actually less effective than telling these voters what was needed to help them and America succeed. After all, these were people who chose to be Americans.

How could this be that a man who was so slimed by the national press would avoid the disdain of millions of voters who one would assume would despise him but instead adored him?

The morning after the fateful NBC tape was illegally released featuring a lurid conversation between Donald Trump and Billy Bush, nephew of Jeb Bush, I found myself wondering if the Trump campaign was over. Trump had always seemed to be able to defy political gravity.

It just so happened that I was scheduled to appear on Fox early the next morning. I quickly called the producer to make sure the topic would not be the tape, as I, like so many Trump surrogates, was trying to determine the facts behind the tape. Also, I had been trained that men were not the best surrogates when mistreatment of women was the topic. I was assured the topic would not be the tape.

When I was seated in front of the camera, the topic changed, which is not unusual on TV, but the new topic was the tape. Moments away from being on live national TV with my reaction to this tawdry tape, I did what I usually do. My mind raced to think through possible questions, and I silently practiced answers I would give. I soon realized there was not much I could say besides being uncomfortable with what was said, although also acknowledging that these types of conversations are not unusual when men gather to discuss women.

Before interviews, I usually pray for guidance. I pray to the Holy Spirit for the right words. I pray to the Blessed Mother for her love and comfort, and I ask God to not have me say anything that could lead someone listening to the get the wrong message. Some will see it as ironic that I prayed on this occasion in light of the topic. But I have found it necessary to pray more earnestly when the topics are the most earthy.

The exchange on television was surreal. The male anchor and I started going back and forth. The Democrat joined in, and she soon started to cry, recounting her own experience with inappropriate sexual treatment from men. The anchor and I were at a loss for words. It was awkward. The Democrat woman was weeping, and we were supposed to do what? Argue? Ask follow ups? I just wanted it to end. I tried to offer words of compassion.

I always fear who will be watching.

My phone rang. It was Mercy.

"What are you doing on TV talking about this tape? Men should not be out there. You are benched! Go home!"

There was little I could say to my wife. She was right, of course, but she did not understand the backstory. But it did not matter. I slunk home.

We drove to our farm that weekend, and we discussed the race and what we should do about the tape and our support for Trump. On the way to the farm, my phone was exploding with calls from those I love telling me I must renounce Trump immediately.

We gathered around our quaint kitchen, and I opened a bottle of Virginia wine and moaned and groaned. By the early evening, we had put it all out on the table. We did not want to step away from Trump, but we needed to not condone the tape. The calls from friends and family also tugged at me.

One of our older daughters, who has a keen political sense, was listening in. She cut to the heart of it all: "Dad, you have been telling us kids that Hillary Clinton would do great harm to the country if she won. Why would you do anything to help her win, even if it looks complicated right now?" One of the other girls reminded us that Mrs. Clinton supported "killing babies in the bellies." Hard to argue with that.

Mercy and I looked at each other and agreed. It was full steam ahead. Damn the torpedoes, we were staying in for Trump all the way. No matter what. And in so doing, we would take even more heat. The attacks on Trump did not weaken him, but they cured the bond between him and his most ardent supporters. Every time the ruling political class thought they had Trump in their sights, they were actually making this unique outsider politically stronger as millions of Americans had similar conversations around similar kitchen tables and came to the same conclusion: this man fights as dirty as the other side.

7.

Conscience is always interesting to deal with. Usually, when you make a decision, you immediately feel relief that the stress surrounding the decision is gone. When you make the wrong decision, you almost always replace one stress with a new stress: the one telling you that you are about to do wrong. In this case, Mercy and I each felt like it was a messy situation, but we were doing what we were called to do. Besides, life is messy.

Many of our friends blamed Trump for all the unease in the country. They were wrong. Trump was not the cause of all the division; he was simply the counter to all the insanity of the radical left on full display during the Obama years. Trump was an actual answer to an America increasingly victimized by a media in the bag for the Democrats and powerful elites who danced to a radical tune in order to hang out with the rich and famous and also because they no longer believed in the true nature of America.

The Trump whisperers were large in number and helped carry him to victory over Hillary Clinton. Little did the whisperers know that even whispering would be enough to cancel Trump, America, and everyone who was a part of the Trump administration.

It was clear that Trump did not just represent a gold-plated emergency break to stop the madness of the Obama administration but was indeed the only person who could save America, take the heat, and begin to make the country great again.

—Matt Schlapp

Chapter 18

Hypocritical Puritanism

It began with a question from Fox News anchor Megyn Kelly, whose opening salvo at Donald Trump in the first presidential debate set the tone, and content, for the remainder of the campaign.[1] The tone would be self-righteously moralistic and the content would be sex, sex, and more sex. Kelly asked, "You've called women you don't like 'fat pigs,' 'dogs,' 'slobs,' and 'disgusting animals.' Does that sound to you like the temperament of a man we should elect as president?"

At the end of that debate, after deflecting the Kelly/Clinton tag team hostility, Trump fired back. Here is what Trump said to debate moderator Lester Holt:

> TRUMP: You know, Hillary is hitting me with [nasty] commercials. Some of it's said in entertainment. Some of it's said [by] somebody who's been very vicious to me, Rosie O'Donnell. I said very tough things to her [Rosie], and I think everybody would agree that she deserves it and nobody feels sorry for her. But you want to know the truth? I was going to say something . . .
>
> HOLT: Please very quickly.

---

[1] "Megyn Kelly and the question that changed her life forever," *CBS News*, April 3, 2016, https://www.cbsnews.com/news/megyn-kel ly-and-the-question-that-changed-her-life-forever/.

> TRUMP: . . . extremely rough to Hillary, to her
> family, and I said to myself, "I can't do it. I just can't
> do it. It's inappropriate. It's not nice."

In the six weeks after that moment, the Clinton campaign did little more than try to prove that Donald Trump was not only sexist but also a serial predator, in the style of former president Bill Clinton. The irony of this barrage of accusations was not lost on Bill, as his face showed in the second debate when Trump arrived with a handful of Bill's former sexual victims.[2] The Clinton campaign betrayed no sensitivity to the ironic backwash of how ongoing Trump accusations merely made Bill's long and recorded history of womanizing a legitimate topic of public discussion in the campaign.

But let's move to the larger irony, and the blatant hypocrisy, of the media's attempt to portray Donald Trump as a bad man and morally unfit to be president of the United States. Where to start? Has anyone suggested that, in retrospect, Bill Clinton must have been morally unfit as well, not to mention the many presidents whose mistresses have been brought to light by their biographers? Commonly cited names include Warren G. Harding, John F. Kennedy, Franklin Delano Roosevelt, Lyndon B. Johnson, Dwight D. Eisenhower, and Thomas Jefferson, but there have been more.

In the pre-internet age, these extra-marital arrangements were obviously easier to maintain in secrecy. But we have not mentioned the most brazen hypocrisy of all: the same media

---

[2]   Charlotte Alter, "Donald Trump Highlighted Bill Clinton's Accusers at Debate," TIME, October 10, 2016, https://time.com/43 41892/presidential-debate-donald-trump-bill-clinton/.

that bashed Trump for his so-called former "conquests" has itself created a culture that celebrates loose sexuality and marital infidelity.

No one can really be blamed for forgetting the Puritan roots of America. The French political thinker Alexis de Tocqueville commented in 1830, "I think I can see the whole destiny of America contained in the first Puritan who landed on those shores."[3] When you compare American views of sexual morality to most European countries, the impact of our Puritan founding emerges clearly. The Puritans landed at Plymouth Rock in 1620, giving all the American colonies on the northeastern Atlantic coast a Puritan flavor. American culture has always displayed a two-faced attitude towards sexual pleasure—condemning it publicly while many indulge it privately.

Consider this question: How can the sex life of Donald Trump be so troublesome to a nation where the 2011 erotic thriller *Fifty Shades of Grey*, by the British writer E. L. James, sold over forty-five million copies in this country alone, and has become one of the bestselling books of all time?[4] The novel's film version became a national hit, pulling in $45 million over its opening weekend, matching exactly the number of

3   Alexis de Tocqueville, *Democracy in America*, trans., ed., and introduction by Henry Mansfield and Delba Winthrop (Chicago: The University of Chicago Press, 2000), loc. 6668 of 1788, Kindle.

4   Andy Lewis, "'Fifty Shades of Grey' Sales Hit 100 Million," *Yahoo! Entertainment*, February 26, 2014, https://www.yahoo.com/enter tainment/news/-fifty-shades-of-grey--sales-hit-100-million-2343 29650.html.

books sold.[5] The only answer is the Puritan root that remains deeply fixed in our individual and social consciences.

Only such a clash of sensibilities—the Puritan vs. the erotic, for lack of a better word—can create a culture where the liberal talking heads can get away with bashing Donald Trump about his purported illicit love life while working for networks where many of their leading on-air personalities would never survive similar scrutiny. The American Puritan desperately wants it both ways: to explore sexuality and exercise erotic daring while condemning others when they are caught doing it.

> It was the summer of 1993, twenty years after Roe v. Wade, and I was teaching a seminar at the Aspen Institute in Colorado with Mortimer J. Adler. Adler at one time had been the nation's most famous philosopher. In 1952, with Robert Hutchins, Adler had published the *Great Books of the Western World* in fifty-four volumes. His defense of the Western intellectual and literary tradition was way ahead of its time. That defense continued for another forty-nine years until his death in 2001. Adler was often seen and heard in the major media. A series of books later in life, starting with *Aristotle for Everybody: Difficult Thought Made Easy* (1978), brought him another period of widespread attention.
>
> On the day I arrived in Aspen, Adler invited me to a cocktail reception at his home. Excited to be there, I arrived early and found myself alone in the living room

5   Pamela McClintock, "Box Office: 'Fifty Shades of Grey' Tracking for $45M-Plus Debut," *The Hollywood Reporter*, January 22, 2015, https://www.hollywoodreporter.com/movies/movie-news/box-office-fifty-shades-grey-765688/#!.

with Adler and Justice Harry Blackmun, the author of *Roe v. Wade* (1973). What I didn't know was that I was to be a guest of honor at Blackmun's lecture later that evening to commemorate twenty years of Roe.

When Adler introduced me as a Catholic philosopher who taught Saint Thomas Aquinas, Blackmun smiled awkwardly. Before he could say anything, I couldn't help but blurt out, "Yes, I am one of those guys who disagree with your decision on Roe." We all chuckled, as polite people do over cocktails when they disagree, and moved on to other subjects.

When I took my seat in the front row of the lecture hall for Blackmun's address, I looked around. It was clear this was going to be a love-fest for the author of Roe. Women filled the hall and stood in the aisles. They roared when Blackmun was introduced and interrupted every few sentences with loud applause.

After several of these ovations, Blackmun looked down at me in the front row—I was not clapping—and held up his hand for quiet, saying to the crowd, "You need to remember that not everyone here agrees with my decision."

The crowd began to boo; there were a few shouts, and I slunk down in my chair, feeling I would be torn apart if my dissent were recognized. I felt a real moment of fear; the response from the crowd felt that visceral.

Everyone who has served in the pro-life cause has stories like this. They may not have ever met Justice Blackmun, but they have looked in the faces of those who justify the murder of children in the name of freedom of "choice," of the right to "control their bodies," to combat "overpopulation" and so-called global warming; the list goes on and on.

But as I look back, the fear I felt that evening did not compare to the fright I have experienced on other occasions in the presence of apologists for abortion. One of the first philosophy classes I taught was an ethics class at Mercer University in Atlanta, a Southern Baptist college. Abortion was on my syllabus, and when that day came, a female student in her mid-thirties with two small children gave a presentation. I can remember what she said almost verbatim. She ended her report, a defense of abortion, with these words: "Before I had my two children, I aborted two others because my husband and I didn't want them. I did it because I loved them, and they wouldn't be happy."

"Because I loved them." The fear I felt at the moment then was far deeper than what I'd experienced that evening in Aspen. Anger can always be turned against those who support abortion; it weakens their argument and suggests a lack of certainty. But love? And happiness? How many people, I asked myself then, have been convinced that abortion is a moral good by an appeal to love and happiness? It's a lie, of course. But Goebbels spoke of the power of the big lie: "If you tell a lie big enough and keep repeating it, people will eventually come to believe it. The lie can be maintained only for such time as the State can shield the people from the political, economic and/or military consequences of the lie. It thus becomes vitally important for the State to use all of its powers to repress dissent, for the truth is the mortal enemy of the lie, and thus by extension, the truth is the greatest enemy of the State."[6]

Most people are only familiar with the first line of that quote. But it's the rest of the quote that makes it so compellingly relevant. The lie can only be maintained if the state represses all disagreement. Isn't that what we have so long experienced in this country? President Donald Trump finally fought back against so many of these big lies.

When I heard my student using love as a justification for abortion, I was a freshman philosophy professor. I knew the "great ideas" had been taken away from us, had been torn from their roots. Ideas like love and happiness were being turned inside out to justify the worst of human crimes: the murder of innocent life.

More than a decade later, I published a book on happiness[7] attempting to trace the evolution of this philosophical mistake. That book was encouraged by Adler himself, who knew that I was using it to address the abortion debate. In spite of his conversion to Christianity, and his advocacy of Catholic philosophy, Adler supported Roe. Every time I pressed him—or Blackmun, for that matter—for deep intellectual convictions about the basis for Roe, the conversation went nowhere.

Adler and I would sit in his backyard smoking cigars on a beautiful summer afternoon in Aspen. I would start the discussion with the Catholic metaphysics of being,

6   "Joseph Goebbels: On the 'Big Lie,'" Jewish Virtual Library, accessed September 29, 2021, https://www.jewishvirtuallibrary.org/joseph-goebbels-on-the-quot-big-lie-quot.

7   Deal W. Hudson, *Happiness and the Limits of Satisfaction* (Lanham, MD: Rowman & Littlefield Publishers, 1995).

act, and potency that he himself had espoused for more than sixty years, only to watch him throw up his hands saying, "Let's not talk about this anymore; I just can't go there," and he would mutter something about upsetting his wife and friends. It's important to mention, however, that Mortimer J. Adler died a Catholic.[8]

With both Blackmun and Adler, I concluded that their support for abortion wasn't really principled at all. Rather, Roe was an intellectually flimsy accommodation to the passions of the feminist movement, passions they did not want to oppose. For Adler in particular, the contradiction he found himself in was painful. He knew that neither good moral choice nor sound laws were based upon mere personal preference or a supposed privacy right.

With the passing years, the rationale for Roe v. Wade appears more and more like the product of a vast sociological experiment: a moment in history when liberal women, aided by compliant men, declared themselves free of creation's order.

—Deal W. Hudson

---

[8]   Deal W. Hudson, "Sed Contra: Mortimer J. Adler, Catholic," (blog), July 1, 2000, https://dealhudson.blog/2018/06/07/sed-co ntra-mortimer-j-adler-catholic/.

CHAPTER 19

Catholics Who Voted for Trump

1.

In 2016, 52 percent of Catholics voted to elect Donald Trump in the face of resistance from some US bishops and despite criticisms from the pontiff himself. A CNN headline announced, "Pope suggests Trump is not Christian" when Pope Francis criticized building a wall on the US-Mexico border.[1] Very early in the presidential campaign, Pope Francis made a harshly judgmental statement about Donald Trump suggesting to reporters that Trump was not a Christian: "A person who thinks only about building walls, wherever they may be, and not building bridges, is not Christian. . . . This is not the gospel."[2]

---

[1] Daniel Burke, "Pope suggests Trump 'is not Christian,'" *CNN*, February 18, 2016, https://www.cnn.com/2016/02/18/politics /pope-francis-trump-christian-wall/index.html.

[2] Eli Watkins, "Pope Francis: 'Those who build walls will become prisoners of the walls they put up,'" *CNN*, April 1, 2019, https:// www.cnn.com/2019/04/01/politics/pope-francis-wall/index .html.

More than a few observers wryly commented that this came from a man who lives surrounded by a two-mile, thirty-nine-foot protective wall. Not to mention the wall was originally build in AD 846, giving popes like Francis plenty of time to take it down. What seemed apparent was this result: Pope Francis, along with some US bishops, were creating an issue that would build Democrats' standing with Catholic voters. This was an issue that would help offset the Republican advantage with Catholics on the abortion issue.

Even Archbishop Chaput of Philadelphia, a longtime hero of pro-lifers, wrote about Clinton and Trump that neither is clearly better than the other. Chaput made no mention of either candidates' position on abortion![3] (More on this in a later chapter.)

Another example was the *New York Times* headline after the pope published the apostolic exhortation *Gaudete et Exsultate*: "Pope Puts Caring for Immigrants and Abortion on Equal Footing."[4] The headline, unlike most on the Catholic Church, is not an exaggeration, as seen in the following statement from Pope Francis, "Our defense of the innocent unborn, for example, needs to be clear, firm and passionate. Equally sacred, however, are the lives of the poor, those already born, the destitute, the abandoned."

This is no mere throwaway line; he reiterates it, connecting the issue of abortion and immigration directly to politics:

---

[3] Charles Chaput, "Some personal thoughts on the months ahead," *Catholic Philly*, August 12, 2016, https://catholicphilly.com/2016 /08/archbishop-chaput-column/some-personal-thoughts-on-the -months-ahead/.

[4] Jason Horowitz, "Pope Puts Caring for Immigrants and Abortion on Equal Footing," *New York Times*, April 9, 2018.

"Some Catholics consider it [immigration] a secondary issue compared to the 'grave' bioethical questions. That a politician looking for votes might say such a thing is understandable, but not a Christian, for whom the only proper attitude is to stand in the shoes of those brothers and sisters of ours who risk their lives to offer a future to their children. Such a thing is understandable."

Pope Francis understands that a political candidate who is pro-life will attract Catholic voters when pitted against a rival who supports abortion on demand. At the same time, Francis insists that America's national borders remain porous for the thousands of illegal immigrants who cross it each month. The context of these statements in an exhortation on the call to holiness suggests Pope Francis realizes the issue of abortion for Catholic voters is not a single issue at all—abortion connects to concerns about the moral dissipation of the culture in general.

2.

Catholics regard a pro-life candidate as someone who will stand against the increasing tawdriness of a culture which mocks religion and puts deviance on display. In other words, a pro-life candidate resonates with the still socially conservative America.[5]

---

[5]   This article contains an early prediction that Trump would win the Catholic vote: Deal Hudson, "Will Pro-Life Catholic Vote for Donald Trump?" *The Christian Review*, February 21, 2016, https://thechristianreview.com/will-pro-life-catholics-vote-for-donald-trump/.

In 2016, Catholic voters rocked the liberal, Democrat-aligned, Catholic establishment by ignoring the nonstop attacks on Trump and his wall by Catholic bishops, priests, nuns, professors, and journalists. Indeed, their voices chimed in with the same message throughout the campaign: Immigration is a life issue, putting it on par with the defense of innocent life. Pope Francis's statement seemed to codify that message. But it didn't succeed; here's why.

Francis's apostolic exhortation ignores the basic moral problem in equating immigration with abortion: prudential judgment. Even the bishops' document "Welcoming the Stranger Among Us" contains no single right or wrong answer.[6] Should Catholics support the "catch and release" immigration policy ordered by President Obama? Or should they support enforcing existing congressional laws pertaining to entering the United States? What about building walls? No Church teaching or single fundamental principle obligates a Catholic to affirm one specific answer to these questions of public policy. On the other hand, the question about whether to abort or not to abort has only one answer—no. Abortion is not a prudential matter.

Certainly, Pope Francis is right about this: at a general level, both abortion and immigration do meet on equal ground—the principle of loving one's neighbor. But that moral equality doesn't confer equality on the type of moral

---

6   "Welcoming the Stranger Among Us: Unity in Diversity," USC-CB, November 15, 2000, https://www.usccb.org/committees/pas toral-care-migrants-refugees-travelers/welcoming-stranger-among -us-unity-diversity.

judgments Catholics are obliged to make. One of these questions is liable to a variety of answers; the other is not.

Pope Francis's statements against Donald Trump on immigration have served to prop up Catholic Democrats who continue to promote abortion, support government funding of Planned Parenthood, and ignore the Church's teaching on life. And yet, his apostolic exhortation does not change Catholic moral teaching on the paramount importance of protecting the unborn because the claim the pope is trying to make cannot be rationally defended. In spite of the anti-Trump headlines, the pope's effective gift to the Democrats did not succeed in alienating Trump from Catholic voters.

During the 2016 election, I watched with disbelief as all but a few Catholic bishops said nothing—in complicit silence—as Hillary Clinton, aggressively pro-abortion, ran for president.[7] Instead, I watched bishops attack Donald Trump on immigration and his promise to build a wall on the Mexican border.

Catholic voters repudiated Hillary Clinton's abortion candidacy nonetheless by voting 52 to 45 percent for Trump-Pence.[8] As an election issue, immigration was trumped by national security, ISIS terrorism, jobs,

---

[7]   Deal Hudson, "Catholics and the 2016 Election – We've Hit Rock Bottom," The Christian Review, September 23, 2016, https://the christianreview.com/catholics-and-the-2016-election-weve-hit-ro ck-bottom/.

[8]   Jessica Martinez and Gregory A. Smith, "How the faithful voted: A preliminary 2016 analysis," Pew Research Center, November 9, 2016, https://www.pewresearch.org/fact-tank/2016/11/09/how -the-faithful-voted-a-preliminary-2016-analysis/.

NAFTA, abortion, religious liberty, but most of all, by patriotism. Most Catholic voters had finally had enough of Barack Obama's America-bashing and saw Hillary Clinton as continuing to blame America for the world's ills.

There was no group of leaders more shocked by the election outcome than those US bishops and their primary supporters on the Catholic Left, including Catholic colleges and universities, many women's and men's religious orders, liberal Catholic media, Catholic Democrats in Congress, and Soros-funded groups such as Catholics In Alliance With the Common Good.[9]

But post-election, many of the Catholic bishops did not learn any lessons from the election results. They have virtually ignored the fact that President Trump wasted no time in keeping his pro-life promises: reaffirming the Mexico City Policy, banning the use of federal funds for abortions overseas, nominating three ostensibly pro-life judges for the Supreme Court (100 percent voted in support of Texas's heartbeat bills), and encouraging Congress to bring a bill defunding Planned Parenthood to his desk for signing.

Instead, many bishops continued bashing Trump, now president, over immigration. As prominent theologian and journalist Thomas Williams wrote about Chicago Cardinal Blaise Cupich: "Saying this is a 'dark moment in U.S. history . . . undermines the moral authority of the episcopate that should know better than to issue

---

[9]   "Soros-Funded Catholic Left Is Dishonest," Catholic League, October 20, 2016, https://www.catholicleague.org/soros-funded-cat holic-left-is-dishonest-3/.

careless statements of the sort. Catholics, and indeed all citizens, deserve better."[10]

Cardinal Cupich, along with San Diego Bishop Robert McElroy, have become leaders of the Catholic Left among the bishops. It was Bishop McElroy who took the pains to point out how Catholic voters would be justified to ignore Hillary Clinton's pro-abortion stance. Those who focus on "intrinsic evil," he wrote, are "simplistic" and "misleading."[11]

At the time, I noticed the irony that McElroy's column was published only days after the canonization of Saint Teresa of Calcutta. Given that Saint Teresa is considered by Americans the "most admired person" of the twentieth century,[12] Bishop McElroy's attempt to scoff at pro-lifers not only failed but has also contributed to the bishops' loss of moral authority.

When bishops as popular and staunchly pro-life as Archbishop Chaput of Philadelphia and Cardinal Dolan of New York City continued to pound on President Trump about immigration, ignoring his pro-life

---

[10]   Thomas Williams, "Why Catholics Need to Take a Deep Breath Over Trump's Migrant Ban," *The Christian Review*, February 3, 2017, https://thechristianreview.com/why-catholics-need-to-take-a-deep-breath-over-trumps-migrant-ban/.

[11]   Robert W. McElroy, "The Greatness of a Nation," *The Valley Catholic*, September 16, 2016, https://tvc.dsj.org/2016/09/16/the-greatness-of-a-nation/

[12]   Frank Newport, "Mother Teresa Voted by American People as Most Admired Person of the Century," *Gallup*, December 31, 1999, https://news.gallup.com/poll/3367/mother-teresa-voted-american-people-most-admired-person-century.aspx.

achievements, just as in the election, the bishops were the losers.[13]

—Deal W. Hudson

---

[13]   Charles Chaput, "Archbishop Chaput's Weekly Column: Persons First: Refugees, Immigrants and Executive Orders," Archdiocese of Philadelphia, January 31, 2017, http://archphila.org/archbis hop-chaputs-weekly-column-persons-first-refugees-immigrants -and-executive-orders/.

Chapter 20

Woke Capitalism

1.

Corporations are profit-driving machines. Concepts like corporate responsibility traditionally were used to promote respect for other employees as everyone labored to drive toward greater profitability for the company. Employees also knew that breaking the law or skirting environmental regulations would breach a corporate culture that understood that going through investigations would distract the drive for efficiency and customer satisfaction.

All this sounds great, and like a real throwback, but corporations were always vulnerable to a pitchman both inside and outside who wanted customers or investors to believe that the company was not only making money but also making a difference in society. We can all remember companies that sponsored television shows or associated themselves with motherhood and apple pie. General Electric sponsored speeches and ads featuring Ronald Reagan and his boosterism of American principles, and there's the local example of the car dealership sponsoring your local tee-ball team with the corporate logo on the children's uniforms.

Now we have Disney and other corporations openly touting Planned Parenthood and abortion extremism, which tragically results in a lot fewer kids ever getting a chance to wear a ball jersey. The worst example of woke capitalism is climate change hysteria. The global elites have been pushing various versions of climate change regulations since the 1980s. Bill Clinton and his pantheist vice president Al Gore famously pushed a BTU tax (a tax on energy use), or a fee to use fossil fuels. The public backlash to such ideas helped the GOP capture Congress in a historic wave in 1994.

However, the history books usually discuss the 1994 GOP landslide as resulting from Hillary Clinton's effort to nationalize healthcare. Why does the drive to punish fossil fuels, which is enduringly unpopular when put into legislative language, always hang around like an unholy Lazarus?

2.

Corporations have for almost forty years tried to manage radical environmentalists instead of trying to minimalize them by discrediting them. This is also true of other radical-left efforts. They may mock them when doors are closed, and hate them during proxy fights at shareholder meetings, but in media interviews and meetings, they almost always embrace commonality.

It is difficult to attack corporations for their desire to make nice with those attacking their products, because the Left has so effectively learned the art of the shakedown con. And the Left has always viewed big corporations and the Church as their two enemy targets. Most mainline Protestant churches and too many Catholic bishops gave up fighting the Left long ago and now embrace similar policy goals. The more that elites embrace the Left, the more they get comfortable with helping them financially, which allows the shakedown to be better funded and which expands targets and enhances the talent and years-long efforts to make change.

We have all been taught to form our individual consciences to avoid associating with those who tempt us into sin or are a bad influence. Unfortunately, the same is true for corporations: once they embrace goals contrary to truth, they violate their corporation responsibility goals and eventually cause the cancer of extremism to spread to similar companies which then feel pressured to follow suit. Are we at a moment when it simply takes one highly respected CEO to stand up and say no? So far, we can relate that behind the scenes, such courage is exhibited, but we have yet to see public leadership push back on leveraging corporations to accept the mandated role of bandleader to destroy the family, the Church, and other institutions on which our society is based in order to get acclaim for tolerance.

3.

Back to our example on climate change hysteria and its enduring ability to be on the political agenda despite its shaky standing scientifically and its impressive list of political setbacks. Climate hysterics come in a variety of categories, including very well-meaning students and young people who have swallowed decades of propaganda that being in the fight on climate change is simply like being against ethnic cleansing or embracing recycling.

What well-meaning proponents have not been told is that the push to eradicate fossil fuels is about controlling our output of greenhouse gases, and of course the biggest driver to CO_2 output is God's creations of men and animals.[1] Therefore, the very nucleus of climate change hysteria is the Malthusian goal of population control through contraception, abortion, and, in turn, the inevitable result of encouraging young men to avoid marriage and fatherhood and pursue the self-actualized life.[2] How tragic.

We have met many men who have regretted a failed marriage, but we have not met many who ever regretted starting a family. In fact, many will regret, especially in older stages, having started a family too late or being convinced that "one of each kind" (one son and one daughter) was sufficient. The constant campaigns (often subtly) in popular culture dinging marriage and family are probably a bigger menace for our society than ending the lives of children legally through abortion, as one is the result of the casual evil of the other.

So why do corporations even get close to such controversial topics at the heart of climate change hysteria? Because they fund the groups that hire the New York and Hollywood creative talent to constantly market climate change in a way

---

[1]   "Where Does Carbon Dioxide Come From?" Reference, March 26, 2020, https://www.reference.com/science/carbon-dioxide-come-85f591a4711a3b97.

[2]   Thomas Robert Malthus (1766–1834) was an English clergyman who became an influential economist: see https://www.intelligenteconomist.com/malthusian-theory/.

where it is the new little league team uniform on which every smart businessman wants his logo.

4.

When President Obama decided to push climate change through its latest marketing brilliance—that is, under the policy label of "cap and trade,"[3] which was a language used because it sounded like a legitimate business deal—corporations affected by it either ducked opposition or opposed it through third parties. And many publicly embraced a legislative "solution" to ending our reliance on fossil fuels.

There were aggressive opponents, but the corporations who would have been negatively impacted were hoping that those in the oil industry would write the checks to defeat it. The legislation was defeated, but the cause of the extreme environmentalists was enhanced as along the way they were able to threaten even more companies and elite voices to publicly embrace their radical goals of exponentially higher energy prices for Americans and their employers.

Our goal in writing this book is not just to identify the efforts of the desecrators to reimagine America by first destroying the effective structures created some 250 years ago but also to offer new tactics. Any young person reading these words who loves God and pledges allegiance to America, or who has a vocation for business, should understand that true leadership means being wily when it comes

---

[3]   Cap and trade is a common term for a government regulatory program designed to limit, or cap, the total level of emissions of certain chemicals, particularly carbon dioxide, as a result of industrial activity.

to challenging opponents. Like great generals, sometimes the wise approach is to avoid the enemy until finding a place to challenge it when the odds of success are higher. However, if General George Washington had never engaged the redcoats, we would have waited 250 years for our Brexit. In other words, always accommodating eventually means you may survive but you will never win and be independent.

Companies that constantly appease the Left, especially its current ugly form of embracing Marxism, socialism, secularism, and outright hostility to faith, family, gender, and childhood, will eventually hire so many people to cajole these hateful groups that they will inevitably morph into public/private partnerships like public television. When this happens, America will have to surrender the role of economic leader to China, which is probably behind the efforts of the Left in America to destabilize what has made her great.

5.

We need to begin to pool together our consumer power. We are fully half the country, and we have majorities in most of the large states which are becoming mega states with economies bigger than most nations as companies move from hostile blue cities to accommodating red deregulatory structures. These states are growing because Americans are fleeing the dysfunction of an extreme ideology that closes schools and churches and small businesses but always wants our border open for business for anyone.

Companies need to fully understand that the more they appease the radicals, and the more they fund them, like they do with Planned Parenthood and Black Lives Matter Inc., they are simply funding the enemy of their future profits. The companies and their CEO's probably will not step out of their inevitable decline unless consumers demand they return to neutrality and stop embracing the weakening of America. Like all great reforms, this one must be led by us, and we will need to risk a lot. However, the more radicals overtake our institutions and go after our children, the less we have to lose in the fight.

CHAPTER 21

Canceling the Support for the Unborn?

1.

There was no reason to be surprised at the lack of Catholic outcry against the Catholic candidate for president, Joseph Biden, who was enthusiastically pro-abortion. The 2016 presidential election had made us wonder if the Catholic Church really cared about abortion. That election pitted an avowed abortion advocate against an avowed pro-life candidate. Making the choice between them starker, Hillary Clinton had chosen a pro-abortion Catholic senator Tim Kaine as a running mate, while Donald Trump picked pro-life governor Mike Pence.

To make the choice even more clear, Hillary Clinton made the support of Planned Parenthood, the proven seller of infant body parts, part of her political platform. The Democratic Party announced a more extreme pro-abortion clause to its platform than in previous elections.[1] Donald Trump,

---

[1]   Rebecca Downs, "Democratic Party's 2016 draft platform 'goes further' on abortion," *Live Action*, July 19, 2016, https://www.live

on the other hand, had promised to sign a bill defund-
ing Planned Parenthood[2] and published a list of potential
Supreme Court nominees all in the mold of the late Justice
Antonin Scalia.[3]

What did we hear from the leadership of the Catholic
Church in the United States? There was one helpful blip on
the bishop's radar: Bishop Tobin of Providence, RI, asked
aloud if Tim Kaine was a Catholic and concluded that
Kaine's support for abortion, among other policies, "are
clearly contrary to well-established Catholic teachings . . .
apparently, and unfortunately, his faith isn't central to his
public, political life."

On the other hand, one bishop who we and many others had admired his entire career for his pro-life conviction
published a shocking column. Philadelphia's Archbishop
Charles J. Chaput, OFM Cap, wrote on the archdiocesan
website, "Some personal thoughts on the months ahead."
He wrote that between "both major candidates . . . neither
is clearly better than the other."[4] The reasons given by the

action.org/news//democratic-partys-2016-draft-platform-goes-fu
rther-on-abortion/.

2   Steven Ertelt, "Donald Trump Promises: As President, I Will Sign
a Bill to De-fund Planned Parenthood," *Life News*, February 18,
2016, https://www.lifenews.com/2016/02/18/donald-trump-pro
mises-as-president-i-will-sign-a-bill-to-de-fund-planned-parent
hood/.

3   Steven Ertelt, "Donald Trump Releases List of 11 Potential Supreme Court Justices, 'I'm Not Appointing a Liberal,'" *Life News*,
May 18, 2016, https://www.lifenews.com/2016/05/18/donald-tr
ump-releases-list-of-11-potential-supreme-court-justices-im-not
-appointing-a-liberal/.

4   Charles Chaput, "Some personal thoughts on the months ahead,"
Catholic Philly, August 12, 2016, https://catholicphilly.com/2016

archbishop began with the income of the candidates, both being multi-millionaires, and he then argued: "The median U.S. income is about $56,000. Neither major candidate lives anywhere near the solar system of where most Americans live, work, and raise families. Nonetheless, we are asked to trust them."

Ironically, the archbishop pointed out this alleged liability even as most dioceses depend on multi-millionaire donors to meet their budgets. The irony is obvious and the point superficial. The archbishop's next argument cited the "defective ethics," "buffoonery," and "bombast" that "make him [Donald Trump] inconceivable as president." Really? The only pro-life candidate was "inconceivable" as president? This vicar of Christ, whom so many had admired and held up as a pro-life champion, was dismissing the only pro-life candidate because of his behavior and past sins.

Next, the archbishop described the pro-abortion Hillary Clinton: "In the view of a lot of people—[Clinton] should be under criminal indictment. The fact that she's not— again, in the view of a lot of people—proves Orwell's *Animal Farm* principle that 'all animals are equal, but some are more equal than others.'" Fair enough—reasonable people agree with that. But the archbishop made no mention of her being "inconceivable" as president. For Archbishop Chaput, Clinton was apparently conceivable as president, but Trump was not.

Chaput went on to remind Catholics that God does not prefer one political party over another: "But God, by

---

/08/archbishop-chaput-column/some-personal-thoughts-on-the -months-ahead/.

his nature, is always concerned with good and evil and the choices we make between the two." Yet, the archbishop's comparison of Clinton and Trump did not focus on the evil of abortion. Given his reputation, the omission was shocking.

Next, Chaput reminded Catholics that not "all pressing issues [are] equal in foundational importance or gravity. The right to life undergirds all other rights and all genuine social progress." If so, why did Chaput not underscore the issue of "foundational importance" in relation to the candidates or their running mates? If the abortion issue possesses so much moral "gravity," why were the candidates not evaluated in that light?

Rather than fully informing Catholics on where the Clinton/Kaine ticket stood on abortion, the archbishop warned Catholics against the "mobocracy" of social media and advised clarity of thought and prayer, as well as reading the bishops' "Forming Consciences for Faithful Citizenship," and their 1998 pastoral letter, "Living the Gospel of Life." Well, okay, let's read it. Here is what the bishops wrote in 1998: "Every vote counts. Every act of responsible citizenship is an exercise of significant individual power. We must exercise that power in ways that defend human life, especially those of God's children who are unborn, disabled or otherwise vulnerable."[5]

That sort of pro-life clarity was not found among Archbishop Chaput's "personal thoughts." Perhaps no bishop

---

5   "Living the Gospel of Life: A Challenge to American Catholics," USCCB, accessed September 30, 2021, https://www.usccb.org/issues-and-action/human-life-and-dignity/abortion/living-the-gospel-of-life.

of the present generation had supported the pro-life cause more consistently and ably than the archbishop of Philadelphia. Why was it not highlighted here in relation to the stated position of the candidates and their political parties?

It was not as if the position of either candidate was a secret. In the case of Hillary Clinton, her passionate support of abortion on demand was both a matter of public record and expressed conviction. What we heard from Donald Trump were political promises—he had never held public office—but they were convictions that go back a decade before this election campaign.[6]

The message being taken from the archbishop's column was that when Catholics choose between Clinton and Trump, "neither is clearly better than the other." Suddenly, for Chaput, an intrinsic evil seemed to make no decisive moral or political difference in determining which candidate to support.

2.

Chaput was just one of many bishops who seemed to divert attention from or downplay Hillary Clinton's pro-abortion agenda relative to Donald Trump. There are six ways that we believe the Church—most of its leadership, media, and institutions—seemed to virtually campaign for the Clinton/Kaine ticket.

---

6   Steven Ertelt, "Donald Trump Explains Conversion to Pro-Life Side on Abortion," *Life News*, April 8, 2011, https://www.lifene ws.com/2011/04/08/donald-trump-explains-conversion-to-pro-li fe-side-on-abortion/.

First, confusion about the candidates and the issues was either sown or not clarified. Much of the confusion came from the voter guides published by the state Catholic conferences in which all the issues were presented as morally equal. The basic approach of the diocesan voter guides was to provide a list of eight to ten political issues and state the Church's view of them. In many cases, all the issues seemed to be presented as equal in weight, with the result being that Clinton would appear more in line with Church teaching than Trump.

In our view, the bishop's own guide to political participation—"Forming Consciences for Faithful Citizenship"—had been carefully crafted from one election to another to provide cover for Catholics who wanted to cast their vote for a pro-abortion candidate, who was usually but not always a Democrat. The most serious problems began with the 2008 version of "Faithful Citizenship"—with the loopholes of this document carried forth to the 2016 version, creating a useful moral ambiguity providing cover for Democrats. These loopholes allowed Catholics to lay aside concern about abortion and other intrinsic evils.

For example, when Archbishop Chaput began his column with allegations about the characters of Donald Trump and Hillary Clinton, rather than the policies they espoused, he was following the dictate of section 37 in "Faithful Citizenship": "In making these [voting] decisions, it is essential for Catholics to be guided by a well-formed conscience that recognizes that all issues do not carry the same moral weight and that the moral obligation to oppose intrinsically evil acts has a special claim on our consciences and our actions. These decisions should take into account a candidate's commitments, character, integrity, and ability to influence a given issue."[7]

It gets worse. Take section 34, which basically says as long as a voter does not intend to support the morally evil position of a candidate, then voting for him or her is justified: "A Catholic cannot vote for a candidate who takes a position in favor of an intrinsic evil, such as abortion or racism, if the voter's intent is to support that position. In such cases a Catholic would be guilty of formal cooperation in grave evil. At the same time, a voter should not use a candidate's opposition to an intrinsic evil to justify indifference or inattentiveness to other important moral issues involving human life and dignity."[8]

Sections 35 and 36 offered two more loopholes, the former allowing support for pro-abortion candidates if there are offsetting "morally grave reasons," while the latter justifies such a vote if a candidate will pursue "authentic human goods" rather than the "morally-flawed" position he or she holds. We are not making this up; this was the official teaching of our bishops as explained in their own document.

Secondly, many in the Church treated anti-abortion advocacy as politically partisan, amounting to an endorsement of a candidate or party. See what the bishops recommended in discussing candidates in a parish "forum." In "Tips for Conducting Candidate Forums" we read: "Cover a broad range of issues: Focusing on one issue will create the appearance of endorsing some candidates over others. A broader focus will

---

[7]   "Faithful Citizenship 2016," Diocese of Little Rock, October 16, 2016, https://www.dolr.org/article/faithful-citizenship-2016.

[8]   Ibid.

more effectively educate voters and will avoid any appearance of bias."[9] Thus, persons and organizations focused on the abortion issue were quieted or excluded from meetings and conferences sponsored by the Catholic Church through a diocese, a parish, an agency, or an office.

Thirdly, diocesan and parish media platforms were used to send messages burying the abortion issue under the theme of compassion for the poor and the immigrant. Such compassion is important, even necessary, but there is no reason compassion should not be extended to the unborn as well. That this "social justice" compassion is not extended to the unborn is both deliberate and (in our view) usually politically motivated to favor the Democratic Party.

Moreover, the Church leadership, especially in the bureaucracy, seemed to forget that the bishops in 1998 wrote a pastoral letter, "Living the Gospel of Life," which said: "Every vote counts. Every act of responsible citizenship is an exercise of significant individual power. We must exercise that power in ways that defend human life, especially those of God's children who are unborn, disabled or otherwise vulnerable."[10] How many parishes heard these words spoken aloud or read in diocesan materials before November 8, 2016?

Fourthly, parishes offered bait-and-switch tactics, such as holding conferences and forums held under banners such

9   "Tips for Conducting Candidate Forums," USCCB, accessed September 30, 2021, https://www.usccb.org/resources/tips-conducting-candidate-forums.

10   "Living the Gospel of Life: A Challenge to American Catholics," USCCB, accessed September 30, 2021, https://www.usccb.org/issues-and-action/human-life-and-dignity/abortion/living-the-gospel-of-life.

as "Respect Life" but devoted to social justice issues with barely a mention of abortion or any other intrinsic moral evil. If you attended, you heard about the lives of the poor, the immigrant, women who have suffered from having an abortion, but you didn't hear any kind of sustained treatment of the Church's teaching against abortion and how it should have been applied to casting your ballot. There were exceptions to this, of course, but the list was short.

Fifthly, at the grassroots level, many in the parishes and dioceses deliberately created obstacles to the pro-life message being used to measure the difference between candidates and parties. Pro-lifers who attempted to hand out materials at parishes typically experienced hostility and discouragement from priests, deacons, and parish staff. Stories of pro-life groups being run out of parish parking lots were many and widespread.

The sixth and perhaps most powerful way that the Church helped the Clinton/Kaine ticket was through its silence. Strict silence was maintained about Hillary Clinton's expressed affection for Planned Parenthood and the celebration of abortion on demand at the Democratic National Convention.[11] In 2020, the bishops maintained the same silence when the Catholic candidate was running for the presidency rather than vice presidency. A few bishops, particularly Bishop Joseph Strickland of Tyler, TX, kept up a steady drumbeat about Joe Biden's unwavering and unapologetic

---

[11]   Irin Carmon, "Hillary Clinton and Planned Parenthood unite after weathering the storm," *MSNBC*, June 10, 2016, https://www.msnbc.com/msnbc/hillary-clinton-and-planned-parenthood-unite-after-weathering-the-storm-msna863186.

support for federally funded abortion on demand. It was only after the election that the better-known bishops began to speak up. It was too little, too late, but perhaps it's a sign of a more courageous defense of life going forward.

Catholic voters need to realize what is going on around them in their parishes and dioceses and challenge the confusion, ambiguity, and silence when they are manifested. The silence, of course, is also evident in the omission of preaching and teaching on our obligation to consider abortion, and other intrinsic evils, in our judgments about political candidates. Indeed, no one needs to wait until the next election to challenge the silence!

CHAPTER 22

Can Joe Biden Claim to Be
Our Second Catholic President?

1.

A central reason the desecrators have become a dominant voice in American politics and society is the failure of the United States bishops in post-war America. No
one group of leaders in our nation have the responsibility
of affirming the sacred quality of all that exists, beginning
with an unborn human life. But for fifty years, many of the
bishops—with notable exceptions, like the late Cardinal
O'Connor—were so aligned with the Democratic Party that
they did nothing to stifle the party's drift toward being 100
percent pro-abortion.

This lack of leadership is especially significant when Catholics make up nearly 25 percent of voters in national elections. Depending on voter turnout, these tens of millions
of voting Catholics in every election have the power to turn
our country in a direction that welcomes life, families, and
more effective help for the poor and marginalized. Most of
the bishops, along with their conference, paid lip-service

to the Church's teaching on life while failing to challenge Catholic politicians with denial of the Eucharist or even excommunication.[1]

In recent years, Pope John Paul II, Pope Benedict XVI, Pope Francis, and the US bishops have called upon Catholics to renew their participation in American political life. That participation means, above all, taking the moral principles of the Catholic faith into the voting booth. It's very clear that one such principle, "the sanctity of life," is not being considered by half of Catholic voters when they mark their ballot. This is a moral failure of the Church in the first rank. This breakdown was never more evident than in the election of a pro-abortion Catholic (if you can call him truly Catholic) as president of the United States: Joseph Biden.

President Biden is on the record for saying he supports abortion "under any circumstance."[2] His vice president, Kamala Harris, could possibly end up taking over the Oval Office sometime in the first term. Her record as a California senator was 100 percent pro-abortion. The Biden/Harris ticket goes on record as the most pro-abortion in US history.[3]

---

[1]   Until very recently, the three exceptions have been Bishop Emeritus Rene Gracida of Corpus Christi, Bishop Leo Maher of San Diego, and Cardinal Raymond Burke.

[2]   Martin Burger, "Joe Biden: I support abortion 'under any circumstance,'" Life Site News, July 1, 2020, https://www.lifesitenews.com/news/joe-biden-i-support-abortion-under-any-circumstance.

[3]   Mary Margaret Olohan, "'Most Pro-Abortion Presidential Ticket In American History': Pro-Life Groups Condemn Biden VP Kamala Harris," Daily Caller, August 11, 2020, https://dailycaller.com/2020/08/11/kamala-harris-joe-biden-abortion-elections-2020/.

Only after the election, sadly, did important bishops, such as Archbishop José Gomez of Los Angeles, the president of the United States Conference of Catholic Bishops, express their concerns about a Biden presidency. "I must point out that our new President has pledged to pursue certain policies that would advance moral evils and threaten human life and dignity, most seriously in the areas of abortion, contraception, marriage, and gender. Of deep concern is the liberty of the Church and the freedom of believers to live according to their consciences."[4]

Archbishop Joseph Naumann, who has a record of being a strong pro-life advocate, issued a statement denouncing Biden's hypocrisy. Naumann, as head of the US Catholic Bishops Pro-Life Committee, has special responsibility for providing Catholic guidance on the abortion issue. Both Gomez and Naumann came under heavy media fire and some snipes from fellow bishops. Naumann, however, became the target of a petition campaign by left-wing Catholics and from a faux-religious organization funded by George Soros to remove him from his committee post.[5]

Archbishop Salvatore Cordileone of San Francisco published a stinging pastoral letter[6] and lent his full support

---

4   Christopher Wells, "USCCB President on Biden Inauguration: My prayers are with new President," *Vatican News*, January 20, 2021, https://www.vaticannews.va/en/church/news/2021-01/usc cb-archbishop-gomez-statement-inauguration-biden.html.

5   Raymond Wolfe, "Soros-backed liberals try to get US bishops' pro-life chair fired for criticizing pro-abortion Biden," *Life Site News*, March 23, 2021, https://www.lifesitenews.com/news/soros -backed-liberals-try-to-get-us-bishops-pro-life-chair-fired-for-cri ticizing-pro-abortion-biden.

6   "San Francisco Archbishop Salvatore Cordileone At Odds Over

to scheduling a discussion regarding communion and pro-abortion Catholic politicians at the June 2021 conference of the bishops. The archbishop was "grieved" when an open letter signed by other bishops urged a delay in the discussion.[7] As two veterans of the Catholic political wars, we believe that the bishops have reached a tipping point in favor of more vigorously defending innocent life.

2.

From the 1980s through the 2000s, pro-life Catholics believed the papacies of Saint John Paul II and Benedict XVI would strengthen the Church's message of protecting innocent life. Both attempted to call out pro-abortion Catholic politicians and the Catholics who supported them, reminding them of their faith's true teaching. As Benedict XVI put it in May 2010, our political action should be undertaken "in a manner coherent with the teaching of the Church."[8] As Cardinal Ratzinger, head of the Congregation for the Doctrine of the Faith, he had written, "A well-formed Christian

---

Biden Receiving Communion," KPIX, May 9, 2021, https://sanfr ancisco.cbslocal.com/2021/05/09/san-francisco-archbishop-salva tore-cordileone-at-odds-over-biden-receiving-communion/.

7   "Archbishop Cordileone 'deeply grieved' by attempts to delay consideration of Eucharistic teaching document," *The Catholic World Report*, May 25, 2021, https://www.catholicworldreport.com/20 21/05/25/archbishop-cordileone-deeply-grieved-by-attempts-to -delay-consideration-of-eucharistic-teaching-document/.

8   "Pope asks Catholic politicians to act 'in a manner coherent with the teaching of the Church,'" Rome Report, May 21, 2010, www .romereports.com/2010/05/21/pope-asks-catholic-politicians-to -act-quot-in-a-manner-coherent-with-the-teaching-of-the-church -quot.

conscience does not permit one to vote for a political program or an individual law which contradicts the fundamental contents of faith and morals."[9]

What happened? It's not that difficult to explain. The US
bishops failed to teach Catholics that the moral teaching on
abortion, like euthanasia, human cloning, stem cell research,
and same-sex marriage, was of a higher order and of greater
importance than other political issues. This importance arises
from there being only one position—abortion is wrong,
without qualification, and therefore all Catholic politicians
should condemn it. Another way of putting it is, abortion is
"non-negotiable."[10]

This confusion has been spread among Catholic voters by
the official documents of the United States Conference of
Catholic Bishops. Since its creation in 1966, the bishops have
released more than one hundred pastoral letters and statements that take positions on dozens of public policy matters ranging from handguns, racial prejudice, climate change,
healthcare, immigration, US relations with Panama, treatment of the aging, farm laborers, and war in the Middle East.

None of these are non-negotiable; they are what is called
"prudential matters."

---

[9]   Joseph Ratzinger, doctrinal note "The Participation of Catholics
        in Political Life," Congregation for the Doctrine of the Church,
        November 24, 2002, http://www.vatican.va/roman_curia/congre
        gations/cfaith/documents/rc_con_cfaith_doc_20021124_politi
        ca_en.html.
[10]   Maegan "Otis" Lindsey, "The 5 Non-Negotiables Explained,"
        Catholic 365, May 16, 2016, https://www.catholic365.com/artic
        le/4293/the-5-nonnegotiables-explained.html.

But during the past three presidential campaigns, pro-lifers have been accused by some bishops and many clergy of not caring about human life after the moment of birth. They are accused, for example, of not caring about immigrants. Pro-life voters are accused of not "welcoming the stranger." This accusation misses the obvious: to be concerned about life is to be concerned about everything. Pro-lifers understand that without existence itself, there is nothing. It's the gift of existence that creates everything.

The pro-abortion crowd is blind and deaf to this fundamental fact of existence. How can anyone "welcome the stranger" if there are no strangers to welcome? How can those persons who were aborted before birth "welcome the stranger?"

We don't know of a single pro-lifer who is a so-called "single-issue voter." Pro-lifers look upon human existence with gratitude, a gratitude that extends from birth to death and beyond. That single issue of life makes all the other issues possible.

The division between the pro-life vote and so-called "social justice voters" is created by a lack of vision and compassion among the latter. Pro-lifers cannot embrace a cause whose purpose is so narrowly defined as to be actually cruel. The social justice crowd, those who abhor pro-life politicians, would let Herod be Herod. How can any bishop or priest try putting a kind face on that? In fact, it's laughable that pro-abortion candidates like US secretary of transportation Peter Buttigieg would wrap himself in the mantle of "welcoming the stranger."[11] Any child in the womb is a "stranger" to everyone except the mother.

---

[11]   Alex Henderson, "Pete Buttigieg: If God belonged to a political

Secretary Buttigieg, like President Joe Biden, will "welcome the stranger" as long as the stranger is crossing our southern border and not a mother's birth canal. From where did this pervasive Catholic perversity arise? Catholic Democrats and some Republicans started embracing abortion as a cause fifty years ago. In 1966, the National Conference of Catholic Bishops (NCCB) and its secular arm, the United States Catholic Conference (USCC), were established. Since 1966, any bishop who wanted to challenge a pro-abortion politico was on his own. They were viewed as disloyal to the NCCB and the Democrat Party.

The story has been told time and time again. But nothing has changed. We have reached the point of utter revulsion. As long as the bishops collectively ignore abortion while cheerleading for open borders, the more the Catholic laity will ignore them and regard them as spineless.

But the wide ranges of issues addressed by the bishops, and rarely about non-negotiable or settled matters, has had a tragic result: few Catholics make the distinction between binding statements of principle and the non-binding prudential judgments by the USCCB on policy issues and its support of specific pieces of legislation before Congress.

Ironically, the bishops themselves recognize the potential for confusion and have addressed it directly, for example, in their 1986 pastoral letter "Economic Justice for All": "We do not claim to make these prudential judgments with the same

---

party, 'I can't imagine' it would be the GOP," *Salon*, May 7, 2019, https://www.salon.com/2019/05/07/pete-buttigieg-if-god-belon ged-to-a-political-party-i-cant-imagine-it-would-be-the-gop_part ner/.

kind of authority that marks our declarations of principle"
(xii). Instead, the letters are attempts to apply Catholic principles to concrete situations. But the authority of bishops,
as they make clear, in matters of faith and morals does not
extend to their prudential judgments in other matters."[12]

An eloquent but rare example of the bishops on the settled issue of abortion is the 1998 "Living the Gospel of Life:
A Challenge to American Catholics," which was published
two years after President Clinton's veto of the partial-birth
abortion ban that passed Congress in spite of resistance from
Catholic Democrats.[13] They wrote about the loss of respect
of human life in America and that no one's life should be
subject to "utility:"

> The losers in this ethical sea change will be those who
> are elderly, poor, disabled and politically marginalized.
> None of these pass the utility test; and yet, they at
> least have a presence. They at least have the possibil-
> ity of organizing to be heard. Those who are unborn,
> infirm and terminally ill have no such advantage. They
> have no "utility," and worse, they have no voice. As
> we tinker with the beginning, the end and even the
> intimate cell structure of life, we tinker with our own
> identity as a free nation dedicated to the dignity of the
> human person. When American political life becomes

---

12   "Economic Justice for All: Pastoral Letter on Catholic Social
      Teaching and the U.S. Economy," USCCB, 1986, https://www.us
      ccb.org/upload/economic_justice_for_all.pdf.
13   "Living the Gospel of Life: A Challenge to American Catholics,"
      USCCB, accessed September 30, 2021, https://www.usccb.org/is
      sues-and-action/human-life-and-dignity/abortion/living-the-gos
      pel-of-life.

an experiment on people rather than for and by them,
it will no longer be worth conducting.[14]

Such powerful eloquence, but as the years passed, the bishops, except for a few, completely ignored it. Meanwhile, the desecrators gained a sure foothold both in the Church and our nation. Many Catholics, but too few, have learned to never wait for the bishops to lead where a settled Catholic teaching is being ignored.

Human Rights

The notion of human rights follows from human dignity: natural rights—the rights that precede any government or society—are the privileges or powers that we have the duty to respect so that all persons can seek genuine happiness in this world and the next. Politicians differ on whether these rights require the government to fulfill them or merely protect the rights of individuals and groups to access them. Please read closely this paragraph from the *Catechism of the Catholic Church*: "These [human] rights are prior to society and must be recognized by it. They are the basis of the moral legitimacy of every authority: by flouting them, or refusing to recognize them in its positive legislation, a society undermines its own moral legitimacy. If it does not respect them, authority can rely only on force or violence to obtain obedience from its subjects. It is the Church's role to remind men of good will of these rights and to distinguish them from unwarranted or false claims."[15]

---

[14]   Ibid.
[15]   *Catechism of the Catholic Church*, no. 1930.

When Thomas Jefferson used the word *unalienable* to describe basic human rights, his thinking was guided by this principle: "These [human] rights are prior to society and must be recognized by it."

Dominant-Issue Voters

Another way to underscore the importance of nonsense-negotiable issues in voting is to describe Catholics as "dominant-issue voters." Liberal Catholic leaders repeatedly complain that Catholics should not be "single-issue" voters, meaning that they shouldn't vote exclusively on the abortion issue. But it's not necessary to be a single-issue voter to give the life issues the priority they deserve. Catholics should be "dominant-issue" voters.

The Catholic Church proposes a vertical—not horizontal—list of moral and social issues for political consideration. Life issues—including abortion, euthanasia, fetal stem-cell research, cloning, and same-sex marriage—are at the top of that hierarchy. These issues should be considered dominant in determining how to vote for two simple reasons: First, the protection of life—the right to life—is a moral principle that sits at the foundation of morality itself. And it's one of the three foundational rights enumerated in the Declaration of Independence. There could be no right to liberty or happiness unless there was a living person in the first place. Second, the Catholic injunction to oppose abortion is unqualified: individuals are not required or allowed to make prudential judgments of the principle to a specific case. Appeals to private "conscience" cannot override this infallible teaching. In the doctrinal note "The Participation of Catholics in Public Life," Joseph Cardinal Ratzinger writes: "In this context, it must be noted also that a well-formed Christian conscience does not permit one to vote for a political program or an individual law which contradicts the fundamental contents of faith and morals. The Christian faith is an integral unity, and thus it is incoherent to isolate some particular element to the detriment of the whole of Catholic doctrine. A political commitment to a single isolated aspect of the Church's social doctrine does not exhaust one's responsibility towards the common good."[16]

Opposition to abortion, therefore, binds every Catholic under pain of mortal sin; it admits of no exceptions. There is no question, then, that as the dominant issue, a politician's position on abortion qualifies him or her for the Catholic vote. From the perspective of the Church, not all the policy positions taken by candidates are of equal importance. Catholics, by understanding themselves as dominant-issue voters, can preserve the hierarchy of values at the core of Church teaching while not ignoring the legitimate spectrum of issues important to political consideration.

3.

Furthermore, by understanding the dominance of life issues, Catholics will overcome their confusion about the difference between moral principle and prudential judgment. Unlike

---

[16]   Joseph Ratzinger, doctrinal note "The Participation of Catholics in Political Life," Congregation for the Doctrine of the Church, November 24, 2002, http://www.vatican.va/roman_curia/congregations/cfaith/documents/rc_con_cfaith_doc_20021124_politica_en.html.

the admonition against abortion, most of the general principles proposed in Church teaching can be implemented in a variety of ways; it's simply a mistake to assume—as the political left often does—that one kind of implementation is more "Catholic" than another.

One final advantage to the dominant-issue approach is that it can help close the unnecessary divide between pro-life Catholics and "social justice" Catholics. There's a clear continuity between providing someone with food and shelter and the willingness to defend his life when it's threatened. The Church often employs the phrase "social justice" when addressing "the conditions that allow associations or individuals to obtain what is their due, according to their nature and their vocation. Social justice is linked to the common good and the exercise of authority."[17]

The demands of social justice, then, begin with the right to life and end with the right to be protected from euthanasia or the temptation of assisted suicide. It's a tragic mistake to detach the idea of social justice from the protection of vulnerable life: the source of moral obligation to protect the unborn and to feed the hungry is one and the same—the inherent dignity and sacredness of the human person.

---

[17]   *CCC* 1928.

CHAPTER 23

Confusions About
People of Faith Voters

With few exceptions, pundits have ignored the marginal gains for the GOP among Jewish, African-American, and Hispanic voters. In the 2004 presidential election, Hispanic voters showed they are not as devoted to the Democrat Party as is commonly held: George W. Bush received a resounding 44 percent of the Hispanic vote.[1] Much of this support was lost during the vociferous in-fighting in 2006 over immigration.

But the point remains, the Hispanic vote can swing. In 2016, the largest drop in religious support for the Democrats was among Hispanic Catholics, which was down 8 percent.[2] In 2020, President Trump won 32 percent of Hispanic votes, once again demonstrating the potential of GOP appeal among those voters.[3]

---

[1] "U.S. President / National / Exit Poll," *CNN*, accessed September 30, 2021, https://www.cnn.com/ELECTION/2004/pages/results/states/US/P/00/epolls.0.html.

[2] Jessica Martinez and Gregory A. Smith, "How the faithful voted: A preliminary 2016 analysis," Pew Research Center, November 9, 2016, https://www.pewresearch.org/fact-tank/2016/11/09/how-the-faithful-voted-a-preliminary-2016-analysis/.

[3] "Exit Polls," *CNN*, accessed September 30, 2021, https://www

Among African American voters, Republican gains are not yet reflected in presidential elections, where Democrat loyalty remains strong, between 87 and 89 percent. Tim Scott (R-SC) is the only black Republican in the Senate but has a highly visible role in the GOP. Burgess Owens of Utah and Byron Donalds of Florida are black Republicans elected to the 117th Congress in 2020. In the media, Candace Owens, former HUD secretary Ben Carson, and former secretary of state Condolezza Rice remain familiar faces.

Jewish voters are generally Democrat loyalists, but 25 percent of them are solidly Republican. But with the Biden administration's horrendous treatment of Israel, we can predict that number will grow. In the 2020 election, 31 percent of Jewish voters supported Donald Trump.[4]

Evangelical voters have become the ground troops of the Republican Party. In the last five presidential elections, the percentage of Evangelicals supporting the GOP candidate has been 78 percent, 74 percent, 78 percent, 81 percent, and 81 percent. Pro-life Catholics can be grouped together with Evangelicals as political activists—they are often found working together in groups like the Susan B. Anthony List, the Faith and Freedom Coalition, and CPAC. In both 2016 and 2020, Trump won the Catholic vote by 52 percent and 50 percent. As a result, those of us who have worked with the Republican Party over the years are encountering fewer obstacles to a robust outreach to Evangelical and Catholic voters.

.cnn.com/election/2020/exit-polls/president/national-results.

[4]   Daniel A. Cox, "The 2020 religion vote," Survey Center on American Life, November 6, 2020, https://www.americansurveycenter .org/the-2020-religion-vote/.

The Catholic vote, however, remains the most potentially powerful swing vote in the US electorate. However, hardly an election goes by without something silly published in the media about the "Catholic vote." The headline "There Is No Catholic Vote" is always seen supported by the same mis-assumption—that there is a Catholic "voting block." There is no Catholic vote in the sense of a bloc of voters that reliably supports a specific set of policies or one political party. Catholics cannot fall for this kind of headline, which can undermine the determination to evangelize the culture and challenge the desecrators.

The key to understanding the importance of the Catholic vote is this: a substantial number of Catholic voters in many states who have historically demonstrated they will respond positively to a socially conservative candidate, regardless of their party identification. In other words, in any given election, a percentage of Catholic voters, anywhere from, say, 1 percent to 10 percent, will vote for a candidate who is socially conservative, meaning pro-life, outwardly patriotic, and supportive of traditional families. These kinds of percentages, even at the lower level, can swing enough voters to produce surprising results.[5]

Our electoral history since the 1950s shows that Catholics who attend Mass regularly vote more often and express heightened concern for issues at the core of Catholic social

---

[5]   See the November 1998 issue of *Crisis Magazine*, which directly impacts the outcome of the 2000 presidential election: "The Catholic Vote—A Special Report: The Mind of the Catholic Voter," *Crisis Magazine*, November 1, 1998, https://www.crisismagazine.com/1998/the-catholic-vote-a-special-report-the-mind-of-the-catholic-voter.

teaching. The more politicians begin to notice that there are millions of religiously active Catholics who vote their values, the more Catholics will have an opportunity to influence their leaders. The true political meaning of the "Catholic vote" refers to those "swing" Catholic voters who can elect a president by their impact on key states such as Florida, Ohio, Colorado, Pennsylvania, Nevada, and New Mexico. Therefore, we're not talking about a Catholic voting "block" but about the 1 to 10 percent of Catholic voters in various states who can win that state's electoral votes for a pro-life presidential candidate.

In our years of working with Catholic voters, we are constantly confronted with some basic misunderstandings among Catholics about political participation. These misunderstandings both diminish their political participation and mislead the voters.

1. The Church teaches that the main responsibility for political engagement and participation lies with the laity, not the bishops or clergy.[6] Pro-life Catholics involved in politics since *Roe v. Wade* (1973) always hear laymen and women complaining about what the bishops haven't done. They have a good point, but the complaint in some ways misses the point—every individual Catholic has a duty to engage in politics beginning with faithfully casting a ballot. *Gaudium et*

---

6   Joseph Ratzinger, doctrinal note "The Participation of Catholics in Political Life," Congregation for the Doctrine of the Church, November 24, 2002, http://www.vatican.va/roman_curia/congre gations/cfaith/documents/rc_con_cfaith_doc_20021124_politi ca_en.html.

Spes, a central document of Vatican II, put the matter strongly: "The Christian who neglects his temporal duties, neglects his duties toward his neighbor and even God, and jeopardizes his eternal salvation."[7]

2. Catholics who vote should not worry about the charge of "imposing" their values on others. Catholics do not seek laws requiring citizens to attend Mass or observe Lenten fasts. On the contrary, Catholics seek the protection of basic human rights through legislation and policy, such as the right to life and the right to educational freedom. Laws and policies embody the values we—as a nation—agree to live by. The principle of the right to life, though taught by faith, can be understood and defended by natural law reasoning alone.[8] The important doctrinal note on Catholic political participation reads: "The social doctrine of the Church is not an intrusion into the government of individual countries. It is a question of the lay Catholic's duty to be morally coherent, found within one's conscience, which is one and indivisible. There cannot be two parallel lives in their existence: on the one hand, the so-called 'spiritual life', with its values and demands; and on the other, the so-called 'secular' life, that is, life in a family, at work, in social responsibilities, in the responsibilities

---

[7] Pope Paul VI, pastoral constitution *Gaudium et Spes* (December 7, 1965), no. 43.

[8] One of many excellent arguments on this point can be found here: Howard Kainz, "Natural Law and Abortion," *Crisis Magazine*, January 6, 2010, https://www.crisismagazine.com/2010/natural -law-and-abortion.

of public life and in culture."

3. Thus, Catholics should know there is no need to leave any part of their faith outside of the voting booth. The much-discussed dichotomy between that part of the Catholic faith that is "personal" and that which is "public" is a fiction, a convenient cover for Catholic politicians who want to support abortion and same-sex marriage without appearing to ignore Church teaching. When Governor Mario Cuomo spoke at the University of Notre Dame in 1984 in defense of this dichotomy, he was effectively giving a green light to Catholic politicians to embrace abortion on demand.[9] Cuomo argued:

> Ultimately, therefore, the question "whether or not we admit religious values into our public affairs" is too broad to yield a single answer. "Yes," we create our public morality through consensus and in this country that consensus reflects to some extent religious values of a great majority of Americans. But "no," all religiously based values don't have an a priori place in our public morality. The community must decide if what is being proposed would be better left to private discretion than public policy; whether it restricts freedoms, and if so to what end, to whose benefit; whether it will produce a good or bad result; whether overall it will help the community or merely divide it.

[9]   Mario Cuomo, "Religious Belief and Public Morality: A Catholic Governor's Perspective," University of Notre Dame, September 13, 1984, https://archives.nd.edu/research/texts/cuomo.htm.

The weakness in Cuomo's argument is obvious: No one is claiming that religious values have "an *a priori* place in our public morality." The question is whether individual Catholics can enter the public square as a people of faith and not have to leave their view of human existence behind. Cuomo sterilizes the question by abstracting it into a matter of "consensus" in the "community." The real result of his argument encourages Catholics never to challenge a moral consensus when it contradicts their faith. In other words, the faithful have to stand back and allow the pro-abortion forces to create the consensus and to shape laws. Why? For the reason that these abortion proponents do not have religious beliefs informing their view of human life.

The question Governor Cuomo never answered is this: why should an atheist have a privileged place at the political table? This makes no sense, especially when you recall that every founder and framer believed in God and the natural law.

But Cuomo's division of the conscience in public and private spheres has haunted Catholic voters ever since. Cuomo's pro-abortion son, Andrew Cuomo, who also became governor of New York, is an example of his legacy. No person can simultaneously serve two versions of the common good; one will inevitably rule out the other. In the case of both Cuomos, father and son, the common good became doing whatever is needed to provide the means for mothers to murder their children.

After a large Catholic dinner in New York City, I got into the elevator of the Waldorf Astoria Hotel to ride up to my room. Before the door opened, two men walked in: Governor Mario Cuomo and Cardinal John Joseph

O'Connor. Only a few months earlier, the cardinal had publicly threatened to excommunicate the governor.[10]

There was an initial chill in the elevator air. I knew and greeted Cardinal O'Connor, and the outgoing Governor Cuomo introduced himself to me. I held my breath. Cuomo was the first to speak, complementing the cardinal's remarks. I don't recall O'Connor's exact words, but they were something to effect that he wished the Catholic governor would change his mind about protecting the unborn. Cuomo, I think, was expecting this parry and responded with a lighthearted, "We should talk about this some time." Cardinal O'Connor did not smile back, nor did he think the offer was a serious one. All he would say in return is that he "would be praying" for the governor. Nine years later, I would get to know the cardinal a bit better when I met with him in the New York chancery. I had made an appointment to ask for his advice about leading the outreach to Catholic voters for the 2000 Bush/Cheney ticket. I began by explaining, "As you know, Eminence, I am the head of a Catholic nonprofit (*Crisis Magazine*), and I am unsure I should be leading such a partisan effort." I don't think I had quite finished the sentence when the cardinal cut in a said point blank, "You must do it, and you must win!"

—Deal W. Hudson

---

[10]   Kenneth L. Woodward, "An Archbishop Rattles A Saber," *Newsweek*, June 24, 1990, https://www.newsweek.com/archbishop-rattles-saber-206234.

CHAPTER 24

What Organizations Are
Willing to Stand and Fight?

This book has relayed very personal examples of the pain associated with standing for truth and being canceled for it. Those who read this book understand because those in their families have experienced similar persecutions.

We now have an alarming trend when it comes to elite opinion in America and globally. A handful of thought leaders, mostly secular, determine what is truth and mete out punishments for those who dissent. We have discussed in detail how *the truth* behind Black Lives Matter was obfuscated and sanitized to make its radicalism more palatable. The goal of the marketers behind BLM was to make the campaign noncontroversial so that every minivan could have a BLM sticker and for BLM to simply be a new way to embrace racial equality.

The major tactic of the evil geniuses who took over BLM is to use peer pressure to get *everyone* to spout the same slogans. Anyone who dissents or stays silent is touted as a racist. They do this to children and teenagers in schools, adults at work, and anyone with a presence on social media. The radical Left is pursuing a coup against America, her dominating culture, and most alarmingly her founding, which cannot be separated from a deep and abiding respect for the role of faith. Those pursuing the coup were emboldened by the success of the BLM extremists through violence and fear.

What we need to recall is that the Chinese coronavirus pandemic played a role in the violence that exploded across America. The virus is a serious threat, but the Left exploits these tragic moments to pursue their angry and radical designs for society. They fan the fear around the virus to shut down schools, illegally shut down churches, and scare half the country so severely that they did not even think it was safe to vote.

We have to ask ourselves if BLM and its destruction of communities and businesses would have ever been able to take hold if there had not been a virus lockdown. When millions of Americans lose their jobs and cannot go to the gym and cannot gather with friends who help keep them on the straight and narrow, including a church, disaster will lurk. We saw this play out before our eyes. And we saw that the legitimate concerns raised by BLM got buried under the extremists who flew its flag.

The elite opinion told us that George Floyd was killed because America is irredeemably racist. They continue to tell us that the various forms of Chinese coronavirus impacting the globe is the biggest threat to the globe. I suppose that the virus is in a death match with climate change alarmism. Instead of presenting the science behind the virus in an unbiased fashion to help individuals make prudent healthcare decisions, these radicalized elites are pitting vaccinated against unvaccinated, sick vs. healthy, and American vs. American. When America faced health crises in the past, entrepreneurism through scientific ingenuity was always the answer. And it is true that government played a big role in these solutions.

Therefore, President Trump's dominant disruptions in pursuit of vaccine options is a historic milestone for which he and his team deserve great praise. Along the way, the radicalized elites tried to take these vaccines and turn them into a political weapon against those who believe it is prudent to study their effectiveness before putting them in the arms of their children. Isn't it ironic? Those voices who have spent fifty years telling us that one should be able to control one's own body on matters of healthcare now threaten Americans who wish to control their individual healthcare choices. Take the case of therapeutics like Ivermectin and other follow on therapeutics that are around the corner. The daily lies leveled against such therapeutics are simply unscientific. Radical politics have taken such a hold on the distribution of medical advice that a drug with few negative consequences is on the verge of being banned and doctors are being shamed for prescribing this drug to those infected with the virus.

Why would a scientific community or those who are well-educated in matters of health not embrace real life human trials with various drugs to learn what works. Unfortunately, that's not the goal of these elites. Their goal is more sinister: to have the government dictate to individuals when and if they should wear a mask, when and if they should go to church, school, or work, and the drugs that they will force you and your children to take to be part of those communities.

The money behind the winners and losers on which drugs or vaccines are pushed by the government is indescribable.

Many companies have profited handsomely from the corporate- and government-induced panic. Sadly, some of the companies fomenting the drive to divide America have been the biggest winners: Google, Apple, Microsoft, Facebook, Twitter, and almost every online giant. And the federal giveaways to drug and medical device companies is akin to the buildup in previous centuries to World Wars.

But the attack on truth, common sense, and individual responsibility has now directly infected our elections and the decisions about who are leaders will be. The virus, riots, and violence resulted in a wave of illegal voting focused on major cities exclusively dominated by a radicalized socialist Democratic party. We voted in 2020 like we have never voted in our 250 year history, breaking democratic norms all to pay homage to Fauci's fictions.

It is not too cynical to use logic to see that the ultimate goal of those pursuing a coup in America want to use any emergency or crisis to aid the cause of electing men and women who agree that America needs to be transformed because America's history is unworthy of defending. It is not a big leap to conclude that the lawlessness that was allowed to dominate most of our big cities in the wake of George Floyd's tragic death was used as a pretext to suspend the election laws later that year. In an age of "my truth," where there is essentially no truth, anything can be justified in pursuit of a goal that is sold on benefitting the transformation of society. How do we know that there is real truth behind election fraud in 2020? With thirty years of high-level political experience, I could walk through all the ways the election was polluted. However, there is a simpler test. The same big tech censors, TV news personalities, and pseudo intellectuals who explained to us that it was racist to claim that the Chinese coronavirus was linked to the Wuhan lab or badgered you about your patriotism or support for the police as being hostile to racial equality are now telling you that if you believe in voter ID, you are a domestic terrorist with racist inclinations.

A trend is now clearly perceptible. It is almost as if the harder they push us to accept something that we have great concerns about, the more we know that little voice inside our head is probably our conscience.

Are we surprised that those who don't believe in God's truth, in sound moral judgments, would obfuscate that truth in order to gain political power? If you can go to Chicago emblazoned in a BLM t-shirt and tell those suffering in the inner-city minority communities that Chicago would be better off without "Western" institutions of strong families and churches, and if those who don't believe in truth are willing to justify the execution of cops, innocent bystanders, and destruction of churches and businesses, what's a little voter fraud? It could be cynically argued that packing ballot boxes is a less violent way to achieve your end goal.

What will the radicals pursuing this coup to take over our country try to push on us next? One thing is certain. They will use every true emergency to result in them gaining political power, and if those who love America are gaining a renewed foothold, as we did in 2016, the Left will use racism or white supremacy as their very first charge against anyone who disagrees with their agenda.

The Biden presidency continues to flounder under a series of radicalized policies that the American voters never fully understood or scrutinized because of the fear, and President Biden is the first American president who was elected yet is perceived as an accidental president. Therefore, his polls, as they continue to slip to historically low levels, could be unrecoverable.

The radicals behind the takeover of America will turn to their favorite charges as the Democrats appear to be losing political power. They will convince Americans once again that there is something wrong with America. They will further divide us, and they will try to prevent the country from achieving a consensus that Marxist policy options are the wrong prescriptions for America. And if they can convince enough Americans that opposing collectivist and statist policies equates to racism and white supremacy, they will accomplish their coup, and the rest of us will have even tougher decisions to make.

In the war on truth, we must decide whether we will we associate ourselves with groups and leaders who back down in this important battle. I have been a partisan Republican since I was a teenager. I remember creating a band for a hat I wore for Reagan and Bush in 1980 (yes, I was that kind of a kid). However, I will refuse to follow a party or politicians who are not leaders in the fight to save America and the decency of her founding. As we head toward another presidential election, I will only lend my support behind a nominee who is battle-tested and ready to fight for America.

I am also a proud Catholic and the father of five daughters. Raising children in these harrowing times is tougher than I ever imagined. When some in the Church refuse to stand boldly for our rights to practice our faith and even go so far as to shutter its doors due to Dr. Fauci's incoherent policies and government mandates, it creates a very real spiritual crisis. I love and cherish my Evangelical friends, and I am glad when the Christian church is flourishing. But it grieved me deeply when Catholic friends of mine told me that they essentially left the Church when it locked its doors due to the panic around the virus. During this time, many Evangelical pastors were willing to risk prison to allow Americans to fully experience their First Amendment rights. When the Church and its bishops and even its pope fails to stand for truth, it fans the flames of doubt in believers. Thankfully, our family experienced wonderful pastoral care. I stay in touch with so many priests and bishops from Kansas where I grew up, and my family has benefited from the love and support of local priests, pastors, and school officials. We feel very blessed to have brave Church leaders in our midst. Unfortunately, I think the confrontations that face our Church leaders will get tougher.

—Matt Schlapp

CHAPTER 25

Whither the Church Now?

I console myself these days with the advice of the Catholic historian Jim Hitchcock. I was on the brink of conversion in 1980 from Southern Baptist to Catholic, and I wrote him to ask what I should think of the post-Vatican liberalizing tendencies among Catholics which John Paul II was so firmly opposing. Professor Hitchcock was kind enough to send me a lengthy letter explaining the difference between the local Church and the universal Church:

> Thanks very much for your letter. I understand rather acutely, I think, the dilemma you find yourself in. I am sometimes embarrassed for my church in its present failings. I think my basic answer to your questions would be to say that when one becomes a Catholic one in effect enters into unity with the Church in its widest sense—not only the geographical breadth that exists at present but also all the ages which have gone before. . . . At the present time one would have to distinguish, I think, between the local church and the universal church. On the local level what one finds is often discouraging. . . . Again, with Roman Catholicism, it is legitimate to prescind from conditions at the local level in order to assert unity with the center.

> This is not an evasion or a rationalization—it is the reality of the Catholic concept of the Church. . . . On one level we may say the Church is concrete and visible. But on another level, I seem to be proposing a kind of mystical unity that obliterates inconvenient specific realities. . . . We give our allegiance to a visible Church, but also know that ultimately our unity there is mystical."[1]

Over forty years later, Catholics are dealing with a "local church," by which I think Hitchcock meant "historical," that has betrayed its basic principles derived from the Word of God. Of course, there are individual exceptions among the laity, priests, and bishops. But the fact that these exceptions appear so clearly is only proof of the pervasive rot of Catholic institutions, their leadership, and much of the laity.

After the election of Joe Biden, whose form of Catholicism perfectly embodies the spiritual rot of which I speak, several bishops issued statements noting the new president's disregard for the innocent life of the unborn. For this, they have been slapped down by a media anxious to enthrone Bidenism as the new standard of Catholic piety. My attitude towards these statements is that they are too little, too late. I am only one among thousands of orthodox, pro-life Catholics who have begged and pleaded for episcopal leadership to confront the "Catholic" Democrats, beginning with Senator Ted Kennedy, who decided that protecting innocent life was a "private affair" and, therefore, beyond legislation.

---

[1]   Deal W. Hudson, *365 Days of Catholic Wisdom: A Treasury of Truth, Beauty, and Goodness* (Gastonia, NC: TAN Books, 2020).

There were heroic bishops such as Cardinal John O'Connor who told Kennedy and his buddy Governor Mario Cuomo that there was nothing private about the decision of any person to take another person's life. Since when did the spatial position of a person inside the body of a mother strip that human being of its right to live?

But where are we now? The pope himself, Francis, effusively congratulated the new president, who immediately gave away millions of dollars to Planned Parenthood and canceled the Mexico City Policy. Pro-abortion Democrats like Nancy Pelosi and Dick Durbin celebrate at the prospect of American Catholics embracing Biden's example. Cardinal Wilton Gregory of Washington, DC, rolled out the red carpet for the president-elect. How can any Catholic look at these men and women with anything but disgust? How can any Catholic not realize that they represent what the historic Church has come to be in 2021? The proudly pro-abortion Catholics are the norm, the establishment, in the Church in our day. How can any Catholic not be scandalized and ashamed?

The way ahead is not leaving the Church or spending all your time lamenting how the historic Church has completely lost its bearings. The answer is precisely what Professor Hitchcock wrote to me about in 1980: we must detach ourselves spirituality from all the "facts on the ground" that defile our faith and reaffirm daily the mystical communion which is our Church. In that Church, stretching across two millennia, the truth of Catholic teaching has not changed: the innocent unborn are persons worthy of being treated with dignity and welcomed into life rather than being slain in the name of "choice."

I won't be paying any attention to Church leaders who have ignored and denied the tenets of their faith for ecclesial success. I will be fed by the Eucharist and by the wisdom and example of Catholics who refused cultural conformity since the Church began, many of whom preferred martyrdom to the world's praise. All of these are to be found still speaking to us from the heart of the mystical bond which is our true Church.

—Deal W. Hudson

CHAPTER 26

Summing Up and Getting Serious

If the great desecration is to be countered, we need to fight back starting now. We have explained in detail who they are and what their goals are. We have related our evidence of the danger to the faithful in America and to the country itself.

Politically, conservatives have excelled at generously funding non-profits that constantly circle and point to the various problems in society. There is value in the rooster alarming us to the rise of the sun. But if the sun were a menace, the rooster would become mundane and annoying.

Certainly, since the historic Reagan victory in 1980, conservatives have believed that the inevitable growth of government into every facet of society could be delayed, and millions of dollars have been raised to build up a firewall so that European socialism or other forms of Marxism would never take hold of American politics.

While many labored to defend American institutions against the Left, our kids were sent to schools, both public and private, that planted dangerous seeds which have germinated to undermine the truths they learned at home.[1] Many

---

[1]   The 1987 book by Allan Bloom, *The Closing of the American Mind: How Higher Education Has Failed Democracy and Impoverished the Souls of Today's Students* was prophetic. The reason it created such

of our kids have literally been taught to disrespect the values of their parents.

Digesting all the bad news can lead to shrugging and saying, "What's the use?" Of course, giving up or standing down will not solve the problem. However, wasting resources in a futile attempt to save America demands serious analysis. We believe that the nation and her faithful are on a razor's edge, and either all could be lost or a whole new defense could be awakened. The election of Donald Trump in 2016 was clearly a demonstration of what can happen. The fact that most never believed it could happen is either proof that American politics is more evenly split or that political miracles do happen!

Here are ten precepts we hope you will take away from your reading of this book. Let's start with the most difficult one to swallow.

It is as bad as you think: accept the new reality so you can change it.

Elites in society are speeding toward cultural changes with abandon. Change has come so quickly that some choose to simply resist the change by ignoring all the damage. It is almost as if by ignoring the deterioration, it will make the evil forces weaker. Or maybe it's a tactic to at least keep you sane.

Instead, the better course is to deal with the reality, as troublesome as it is. No matter what it takes to buckle down and accept the new reality, it is important to get to it. Like taking a swig of whiskey in preparation for pain, only in

---

a furor at the time is simple: Bloom exposed the liberal arrogance in turning education into indoctrination.

embracing the full scope of our new reality can we be wise in countering it.

As much as we do not want to get down in the dirt with the other side, it is critical to understand that the great desecration has, at its core, created great animosity toward the Church, the faithful, and any part of American history that is hospitable to traditional faith for its rejection of abortion and birth control. One might say that even Jesus himself is not immune to the current tactics; after all, he was the first victim of cancel culture. It was not enough to simply dismiss him; we had to demonize and kill him.

Call out the evil and the evildoers!

During a televised football game a few years ago, a Catholic university played a promo that described how students read the Bible and Karl Marx in order to be exposed to various points of view. This was a none-too-subtle attempt to soften a terrible intolerant thug like Marx. Marx hated faith, was cruelly anti-Semitic, was a racist, and should only be studied if the barbarity of his life is included and explained. Why would a premiere Catholic university in America speak of Marx in the same breath with Scripture?

However, the Marx of academia is simply a philosopher who wants to help the working class be equal with the economic and political power of land and business owners. The problem with studying Marx is that his ideas are often boiled down to class and economics when the true evil of Marxism is its disregard of individual human rights and animosity toward anything holy.

Call out the evil and evildoers. Explain the cruelty of their heresies and tell the tragic stories of their victims. Of course, none of us are perfect, but do not let the virtue of humility keep you from committing the great scandal of allowing minds around you to be propagandized. If our heroes continue to be canceled while communists like Marx are soft-pedaled as virtue seekers, we will continue to lose the education war for the minds of the next generation.

Demand transparency.

For too long, conservatives have argued for high principles like the right to live a quiet life with the ability to keep confidential political activities and philanthropy. The right to make charitable decisions without fanfare is certainly consistent with the desire to balance doing good with a human desire to get good press.

The Left has shrewdly targeted and attacked any donors who supported causes they despise. If a cause can be made controversial, the next step is to bring to light all the financial backers. Once they undergo relentless negative media coverage, most conservative donors face either the destruction of their companies or internal family animosity, as the next generation deals with all the consequences of the cancer of cancel culture.

Donors pushing Marxism and nihilism hardly ever receive similar treatment. In fact, the depth of their involvement is only understood when they start publicly bragging. It is also time to expose those funding the great desecration and the politicians doing their bidding. Make them suffer the consequences of the public digesting the full scope of radicalism they fund and prop up.

Reciprocity: Republicans and conservatives cannot be the only political victims.

One of the most crucial lessons from the Trump presidency was Donald Trump's commitment to have his political enemies be held to account. He publicly called for Hillary Clinton to be investigated for breaking the law on her laptops, emails, and government communications. He asked the Department of Justice to get to the bottom of the illegal spying that the Obama administration had commenced on Trump.

Republican lawyers from previous administrations positively winced at what they called his "uncivil" and "unpresidential" approach. Republicans in DC understand there are two sets of rules, as it is a city ultimately run by powerful Democrats. Trump seemed shocked at the double standard and was never going to play by the unwritten rules. It was long overdue. Republicans go to jail, while Democrats go on corporate boards. Donald Trump believed that only when the Democrats are held to the same rules, will they stop successfully using the legal system to stop progress attempted by national Republicans.

The history of scandal is alarming. Since Richard Nixon was first ensnared in the scandal of financial wrongdoing when he was Dwight Eisenhower's vice president, Democrats have used legal scandal either to end the careers of their Republican opponents or simply to destroy their political potency. We cannot think of a Republican president since Eisenhower who has not been through it, and many vice presidents as well:

Agnew: An IRS investigation resulted in his resignation.

Nixon: The appointment of a special counsel and the Watergate scandal resulted in his resignation.

Ford: He lost as the second political victim of Watergate.

Reagan: A special counsel was appointed for Iran Contra in his second term (perhaps the lone political survivor).

Bush 41: He was accused of colluding with Iranian mullahs to prevent the American hostages being released until after the 1980 election and also for abuses associated with Iran Contra; he lost reelection.

Dan Quayle: He was belittled for being an intellectual lightweight, which killed his future political ambitions.

Bush 43: He left office with historically low poll numbers, and his second term was marred by an unrelenting hostility in the press. Although he won a second term, he receded from politics.

Dick Cheney: He was relentlessly accused of everything from profiting off of his role as vice president to being a war criminal. The media referred to him as Darth Vader.

Donald Trump was characterized as an abomination who had an irreverent approach. The coverage was withering.[2] But when you compare the coverage to what President George W. Bush had to endure, one realizes it was the same tactic with a new target. Sadly, former targets do not always seem to understand that.

Even if you do not like a given Republican politician, be wary whenever you read that they are being investigated for

---

[2]   Thomas E. Patterson, "News Coverage of Donald Trump's First 100 Days," HKS Faculty Research Working Paper Series RWP17-040, May 2017.

criminal wrongdoing. Yes, Republicans can be crooks too, but DC is a town run by Democrats, so when national Democrats have power, the two work together to use *all* power to stop opponents.

Republicans try various tactics to avoid the condemnation of the swamp: they support greater funding and autonomy for DC, currently demonstrated by the incredulous attempt by liberals to make DC a state. A slew of Republicans even tried to buy love by publicly chastising Trump. Just look at those former GOP leaders with prominent roles on CNN and MSNBC: these Republicans are not exhibiting courage but are playing a well-compensated roll to help Democrats and hopefully help their careers along the way. This is, as Donald Trump pointed out, "the swamp."

Be open to helping Republicans unfairly caught up in persecution by prosecution. Encourage future Republican presidential candidates to look at aggressive pardons for political victims, remembering that if one is found guilty of a crime that is not directly related to the serious charges, then it was all a game to get a scalp. Let us work together to fund scalp reconstructions! Sadly, America is on a course where many Republicans find themselves being convicted more for their politics than their criminality.

Fight racism, not America.

We can both be strong patriots and fight racism. Bigotry is inconsistent with living a virtuous life, whether it is racism, sexism, or bigotry against people of faith, the police, and the military. However, the race war raging across America is being fought on two levels. There are well-meaning

Americans donning Black Lives Matter shirts and hats because they want to find common cause with victims of racism or maybe they, too, have been victims. The decency of these advocates can help America heal.

However, they are being used as a grassroots front for the more illegimate uses of Black Lives Matter Inc., which is a very well-funded, complex series of non-profits aimed at pushing Marxism and remaking America with the false assertion that because America has had racist laws and practices, she is irredeemable and so are the seventy-five million citizens that voted for Donald Trump in November 2020.

Think about what was regarded as the radicalism of Dr. Martin Luther King Jr. and his message from the 1960s. He called for us to judge men on the content of their character rather than the color of their skin. Today's BLM radicals hardly ever quote Martin Luther King Jr. because he was a proud American but mostly because he was a man of God. Remember, preachers are part of the order to be overturned.

The Republican Party was founded to end legalized slavery. The Republican Party was also a target of the Ku Klux Klan, as were immigrants from Catholic countries. The Republican Party led the fight to pass three civil rights amendments to the Constitution in post-Civil War America. It was the Democratic Party that erected Jim Crow to find a new way to resist the civil rights of former slaves. Woodrow Wilson, a Democrat icon, showed the film "Birth of a Nation" at the White House, a propaganda film about the heroism of the Ku Klux Klan during Reconstruction.[3]

---

[3]   Alexis Clark, "How 'The Birth of a Nation' Revived the Ku Klux Klan," History, August 14, 2018, https://www.history.com/news

Republicans do not have a perfect history on race, but its history is completely unexplained by so many elite institutions like in academia and in corporate media outlets, which both cover the stories of race and fuel the false assertion that the Republican Party is the racist party. History tells us that a greater percentage of Republicans voted for civil rights legislation in Congress in the Jim Crow era than Democrats. This simple fact has almost been erased from those who teach our history. It is time for all of us to relearn our history, to redouble our efforts to fight racism and bigotry, and to always resist the tactic of morphing the fact that racism exists in America into the vicious conclusion that America is systemically racist. Because if that is the lesson our kids and grandkids learn, why would anyone fight for America?

If America is so rancid, perhaps it is time to start afresh and "fundamentally transform" America as President Obama famously challenged. This chaos based on a fabricated history must be countered now.

Unborn black lives matter too.

The just mission of defending the unborn child is woven into the debate on race. The Left loves to equate racism and immigration. Leftists will charge that supporting borders and a legal process with enforcement is just the outgrowth of Republican racism in America, since immigrants crossing our southern border are from Latin America and not western Europe.

However, why is the cruelty of abortion and its staggering impact on the black community never equated? Why

/kkk-birth-of-a-nation-film.

is the racism of Margaret Sanger, the founder of Planned Parenthood, a pillar of the modern Democrat Party, never the prime example of elite whites using money and power to prevent population growth in communities of color?[4]

In politics, it is seldom wise to bring up one controversial topic to counter another. However, it is time to reconsider all the rules of public debate. Besides, the pro-life cause is the one part of the conservative pushback from the sexual revolution that has made constant progress. Perhaps one reason for that progress is that supporting rights for the unborn is not simply conservative, nor is it plausible that a racist would support protecting the lives of millions of babies from a rainbow of races.

Shopping is like voting.

For too long the Left has successfully leveraged institutions and powerful people to join its cause or one aspect of its policy agenda in return for positive public statements from leftist groups. Implicit in this shakedown is that if a target does not agree to the terms of the Left, they will be smeared as bigoted in some way, usually as racist.

We have outlined how major corporations and corporate media have chosen sides by and large against the views of those who love America. What can be done to turn the tide in these elite battles? Remember the power of the purse.

---

[4]   Kristan Hawkins, "Remove statues of Margaret Sanger, Planned Parenthood founder tied to eugenics and racism," *USA Today*, July 23, 2020, https://www.usatoday.com/story/opinion/2020/07/23/raci sm-eugenics-margaret-sanger-deserves-no-honors-column/54801 92002/.

Conservatives need to join the fight with their consumer power and their political voice. Only when leaders hear from the other half of the country will they think twice before entering the political fray.

The online organization 2nd Vote is a consumer guide for corporate philanthropy.[5] A consumer can visit the group's website to see if a particular company is funding the values destroying America. The premise of 2nd Vote is that we do not just elect policies at the ballot box; we vote each time we purchase. One great aspect of 2nd Vote is that it is not just about boycotting bad companies but also about finding alternatives which are neutral on cultural topics. Therefore, we can choose boycotts, or buycotts! It is all up to the consumer. One thing is for certain: the old rule that said only leftists boycott needs to be reexamined.

Now that companies are attacking police officers, voter ID, and basic principles of faith, it seems clear that giving them thousands of dollars is no longer operable. In fact, what we are seeing is a panic in board rooms among people who casually thought that taking progressive political positions would be widely acceptable. Keep up the scrutiny; the pressure is working.

Teach kids to respect religious leaders.

There is no question that one tactic of the Left is to isolate the other side and to make it feel insignificant and powerless. We wonder why a bishop or minister is not being more public on an issue important to people of faith. They may not be

---

5   2nd Vote Homepage, accessed October 1, 2021, https://www.2ndv ote.com.

unsympathetic, but they may falsely believe that their voice will have no impact. This silencing of huge segments of society is crucial for a minority to convince a voting public that their cause is widely popular. Therefore, it is not just about our counterattack or the debate with those pushing the great desecration, it is also equally important to praise those willing to fight them, whether publicly or more quietly. Letting a pastor, a CEO, or a politician know that you support them, especially amid a controversy, will encourage positive leadership.

Our children and grandchildren face a similar battle each day. Do they speak up in class when leftist propaganda is afoot, or do they let it pass? Human beings were meant to be together, and human relationships help when grappling with important issues. Therefore, we must present opportunities for young people to form friendships with pastors, religious, conservative activists, and with those supporting American institutions like cops or members of the military. Young men and women will never consider military service if they do not know adults serving who they can look up to. The same is obvious about living a religious life or vocation.

But those in these leadership positions also feel isolated, and they must now more than ever wonder if they have chosen the right profession. A perfect solution to a new generation being propagandized to fear organized religion and despise America generally is to link the young person with an adult serving to make America and Americans better.

If we can enhance the morale of those leading us, they will lead more courageously. If students can see the sacrifice of so many in society, they will have a greater chance of respecting the cause. Therefore, let us all work to communicate our support to the institutions being desecrated and let us remember that we have a role to play as well.

Take over the management of raising your kids and grandkids.

One of the clearest problems in our country is the reliance on a school system to raise kids when parents, many of them stretched in single-parent households, are working in jobs that require constant attention as smart phones intrude more and more after the office is closed. It was assumed that schools were a safe place where kids would learn respect, academic lessons, and how to socialize. Perhaps teaching was not always a profession that people of all persuasions wanted to attain. Unfortunately, a sharp leftward turn is now unmistakable. The drift is unfortunately not just a phenomenon of public schools, as elite private schools and too many religious schools seem to want to be part of the woke crowd.

Working, busy parents need to get a little less busy, immediately. They need to read syllabi and engage with teachers and school leaders. Teachers and administrators of good intent will welcome a parent's interest. If you experience a frostier response, be alarmed. Oftentimes, students being bullied for fidelity to faith or country will not tell parents. Parents need to both talk regularly with students and be a presence in the school. Parents with more time need to get aligned with parents with less time.

Forming informal meetings with other likeminded parents is essential, especially if a school has embraced all the components of the modern education system, with diversity programming and sessions about "white privilege." Do not be surprised if a school you trust has already complied with many mandates and pressure to achieve accreditation or esteem. Schools are radicalizing with increasing haste, this includes Catholic schools. Caring adults must speak up and organize now.

Teach your kids practical knowledge to be prepared.

Most suburban kids have little knowledge of where their food comes from. Now more than ever students should rediscover nature. They need to understand how things grow and what threats exist for the food they enjoy. The more kids understand nature in all its sacredness, the less they will fall victim to myths about what is really happening with ecology. Understanding the food chain is part of this learning. The move to cities and to the counties that surround the urban core has resulted in millions of people who are unaware of how the staples of life they enjoy come to be available.

The most basic practical knowledge under attack is the proper use of firearms. Guns are dangerous and should be respected. But they are also a part of life, a part of hunting for food, and a necessary component of personal security. Teach your kids to respect and properly use firearms. Find an expert and learn to master shooting.

Get kids to start learning about how their food grows out of the ground and from trees. Get them into the garden. Let them plant and care for different varieties of plants. The more kids see how plentiful, rejuvenated, and undeterred nature is, the less they will fall victim to the panic of environmental extremism. Have them spend a month on a farm;

send them to flyover country; buy them a BB gun! (No, they won't shoot their eye out!)

We exist at this time for a reason. We are here together at a complicated time. However, each generation has its challenges. The major question for Americans who love America and for freedom lovers around the world is whether we are winding down or just in a rough patch. Prayer and hope are at the center of this struggle. In the Catholic churches of the Commonwealth of Virginia, it is now common to say the prayer to St. Michael the Archangel at the end of Mass. It speaks to the moment we are in.

Angels are used in modern décor and communications as plump companions. But this prayer, as well as the Bible, explains the true nature of angels: warriors, messengers, and brave protectors. America needs the protection of angels, and we hope America is worthy of them. For to be one nation under God, free from the tyranny of false gods and demonic desecrators, we need heavenly aid and brave patriots more than ever.

Prayer to St. Michael the Archangel

St. Michael the Archangel, defend us in battle, be our protection against the wickedness and snares of the devil. May God rebuke him we humbly pray; and do thou, O Prince of the Heavenly host, by the power of God, cast into hell Satan and all the evil spirits who prowl about the world seeking the ruin of souls.
Amen.